TAFELBERG
HUMAN & ROUSSEAU

CLEM SUNTER

Pretoria
will provide
and
other
myths

ILLUSTRATIONS
BY MARGARET SUNTER

First published in 1993 jointly by
Tafelberg Publishers Ltd, 28 Wale Street, Cape Town
and Human & Rousseau (Pty) Ltd, State House,
3-9 Rose Street, Cape Town

First edition, first impression 1993

ISBN 0 624 03239 6

To my mother, Gwynne Sunter,
and in memory of
my father, Jack Sunter

Contents

The idea for this book came from a conversation I had with Peter Gallo about the best ways to demonstrate the power of scenario planning in companies. We agreed that one method was to present the company's own official version of its future, and then pose alternative stories which would raise the eyebrows of the audience. This led me to thinking about all the official stories circulating about the present and future which on closer analysis could be considered suspect.

I have provided 57 such "myths" in this book, in each case giving the title of the myth and then the alternative story. Like all the work I've done in the past, I've tried to mix humour with serious intent and to get the intellectual juices of the readers flowing. After all, it's better that readers question their own assumptions and write their own alternative stories, using this book as a prototype.

I would like to thank various people involved in this venture. Firstly, there is my wife, Margaret, who not only typed the manuscript but also produced the illustrations which, as a totally unbiased husband, I regard as an excellent offset to the script. Secondly, Peter Gallo has always been a firm friend and a perfect foil for testing new scenario concepts. Thirdly, Theo Rudman is one of the unsung champions of the informal sector and gave me material for the myths relating to that field. Finally, my two great chums – Koos Human of Human & Rousseau and Jürgen Fomm of Tafelberg – are a principal motivating factor for me to put pen to paper again. One of the myths I describe is "Words are read". I hope for the purpose of the pages that follow that I am temporarily wrong!

Mankind has become more civilised

Really? This century has seen two world wars, the first one killing nearly 10 million people and the second one 55 million. In addition to Hitler's unspeakable Holocaust, Stalin and Mao Zedong were responsible for the deaths of millions of their own citizens. More recently we have had Pol Pot's wholesale massacre of Cambodians. Now we are subject to nightly television newscasts depicting equally sordid atrocities, though not at present on the same scale of human loss. Whether it be ethnic cleansing in Bosnia or feuding between warlords in Somalia or the Mujahedin in Afghanistan, it would seem that man's innate desire to kill his fellow man has not in any way abated. Nor has his ability to stoop to ever more exquisite and base acts of cruelty been impaired.

Aside from war, the level of child abuse and child prostitution, the increase in violent crime, more often than not associated with drugs, and the revival of long-simmering ethnic and religious hatreds defy imagination. It is argued that evil on such a scale has always been around, and it is merely the much greater effectiveness of the media now that has brought it into the public eye. I wonder?

We are mass-producing poverty-stricken people at a rate that has never been experienced before in the history of the world.

We do not know what harm we are doing by pumping gigantic quantities of chlorofluorocarbons and other chemicals into the atmosphere. We definitely know that we are violating certain environmental thresholds on the earth's surface through desertification and through poisoning the rivers and oceans with waste. Despite medical advances which raise life expectancies, old viruses are mutating to stay ahead of the prophylactics that are designed to destroy them and new viruses are being discovered. Tuberculosis and malaria are rearing their ugly heads again. The scourge of Aids is yet to be fully felt in the developing world, but it is already claimed that it will be the largest pandemic ever to afflict mankind.

I am not trying to sound like one of the professional doommongerers. The end of the world is not nigh! But it's a myth to take progress for granted. A very fine balance exists between civilisation and barbarism and the world oscillates between the two. It will need a concerted effort on the part of the major economic players and a fair amount of luck to ensure that the scales tip in the right direction in the future.

We are at the end of history

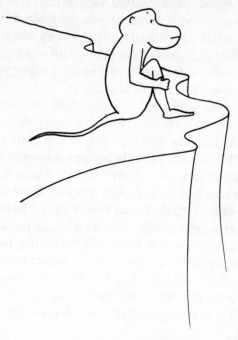

People have a very limited capacity to imagine how the future may evolve over a long time span. One hundred years qualifies as such a period. It is therefore wrong to assume that the present ranking of countries, the technologies that are currently prominent and the ideologies which are now popular will be shaping world society in the latter half of the next century. An oft-quoted phrase at the moment is that we are at the end of history in that Marxism is dead and the free market system has emerged triumphant for all time. Amen.

What a myth! But let us go back a hundred years to see how foolish such a statement is. In the 1890s Britain was still the number one country and Europe was the focus of the world. America was just beginning to get into her stride. The first cars were being driven and the first wireless messages were being sent. Nobody at that time had any idea of how the new methods of transport and communication would revolutionise the pattern of living. Mass-production methods had yet to reach their peak, although the forces concentrating people into large units of production and consequent urbanisation were already evident. Classical physicists were boasting that if they had access to every piece of scientific information they could work out exactly how the world was determined and predict every future event. For them, it was "the end of physics".

Yet, just as the great continental plates drift beneath the world's crust with only an occasional external sign (such as the San Francisco earthquake in 1906), so major shifts in global power and in scientific knowledge only become apparent when a specific event or theory exposes them. The event which demonstrated that America had irrevocably eclipsed Britain as a superpower was its entry into the Great War in 1917. The theory which overturned the determinist view of the universe was quantum physics initiated by Max Planck in 1900, when he suggested that light was emitted and absorbed in separate energy packets or quanta. This paved the way for the principle of uncertainty which proved that unpredictability was an essential feature of the universe of electrons and other elementary particles.

Perhaps we are now witnessing a similar shake-up in geopolitics and science as we approach the end of this century. For, as the spotlight moved away from Britain and Europe to America a hundred years ago, so the centre of gravity of the world's economy now appears to be relocating to China and the Far East. On the scientific front, Stephen Hawking's theory of black holes may completely change our conception of how the universe was created. And maybe we are about to experience a battle of breathtaking proportions between the great beliefs of the world: Christianity, Islam, Buddhism, Hinduism and Shintoism. Back to the crusades?

Some nations have superior genes

History contradicts this myth. No nation has risen to the top and stayed there for long. The list of temporary winners is impressive – Babylon, Assyria, Mesopotamia, Egypt, Phoenicia, Greece, Rome, China, Holland, Spain, Portugal, Britain and America. The latest winner is Japan. Everybody wants to know what makes Japan tick, just as everybody wanted to know what made the British tick, a hundred years ago. Now nobody wants to know what makes the British tick, and it is almost certain that attention will move on from Japan to other Asian countries such as Malaysia, Indonesia and, ultimately, China.

It is a country's leadership, will and value system that drive it to the top. It is the degeneration of those characteristics that leads to decline afterwards. Take Japan and Germany. They both lost the Second World War. They went back to zero. They started from scratch. Over the next 45 years, in different ways, they have both had a glorious run. Now that run may be ending because the latest generation of Japanese and Germans do not share the values and work ethic of their predecessors who emerged from the miseries of the war.

The irony of this cycle of success and failure is that it occurs in individuals as well as countries. Moreover, it applies to all fields – business, sport, music and science. One starts lean and mean. Raw ambition drives one to be excellent and beat the competition. Complacency takes over at the moment of success and thereafter the slide occurs towards mediocrity. Occasionally there are the exceptions of brilliance lasting throughout a lifetime – Beethoven for example. Of course, a country endures longer than a lifetime. Nevertheless, few have more than a brief moment of glory and even fewer a second coming. Italy did it with Julius Caesar and the Renaissance, and China may get to the top spot again, having been there once before in the 13th century.

The conclusion one draws from history is that it is not genes that elevate nations above one another. It is a temporary mix of motivation and inspirational leadership at all levels of society. This may have been preceded by a really traumatic experience which shook the whole nation down for change. On this basis, one could argue that the best prelude to the negotiation process and transition in South Africa has been the deep recession. It has brought people together to survive, it has taught politicians about the folly of making promises when there's little money in the till. It has improved attitudes, a vital precondition to economic liftoff.

High walls will save us

Rich nations believe in the myth that high walls will rescue them from the poor young billions that live in the rest of the world. The high walls they build are not literal as they used to be. One thinks back to Hadrian's wall, the Great Wall of China and the Berlin Wall (the latter having been built to keep the poor in rather than the poor out!). However, the new walls, though not of stone or cement, perform the same role. They are composed of tougher immigration laws, more frequent border patrols, turning boat people back to their country of origin and protecting domestic producers with subsidies, quotas and tariffs against competitive imports from the developing world. In the last category, the most conspicuous example today is the blocking of East European steel and agricultural imports into Western Europe. As one Polish observer commented: "They've revived the Berlin Wall, but this time it has been put around the whole Common Market."

Meanwhile, to seek to pacify the throngs on the other side of the walls, rich nations are throwing handfuls of shekels to them as a consolation prize. It's called development aid. The inhabitants inside the walls go about their daily business with only a faint recognition of the turmoil taking place externally. The suffering has been filtered out. Occasionally, a picture of a starving child in Africa or a mutilated civilian caught in the crossfire in some bloody war somewhere will impinge on the public conscience. Any urgency which such images convey quickly withers when the rich old millions switch television channels to watch the latest super sports event or catch up on the latest goings on in the "soap" of the day.

Even inside the rich nations, high walls are being built by the relatively privileged to guard against their own underclasses. In California the most popular form of residential development is the walled city. For a long time the middle class has been fleeing from the inner urban areas to suburbs and now to country fortresses.

History teaches us that this strategy of exclusivity – of hiding inside gilded cages – is bound to fail. Eventually the excluded find a way over the walls as they did in the Sack of Rome in 410 AD and as they will do from Eastern Europe and Russia if Western Europe continues to pursue its short-sighted policy of protection. A much wiser and more long-term strategy is to reach over the wall and help the poor young billions help themselves by sharing ideas and technology and opening up markets in which everyone can trade. By these means, the people on the other side of the wall will be too busy pursuing their own careers with ordinary ambitions for themselves and their families to consider revolution against the established system. Nevertheless, it is highly unlikely that the walls will disappear altogether, since the world is not ready for universal freedom of movement.

I'm gonna get me a gun

This is the South African version of the previous myth. Once upon a time the rich old millions had influx control and curfews with which to protect themselves from the poor young billions. Anyway, the majority of the poor young billions were parked out of sight and out of mind in the homelands. Now that the walls of separation have tumbled and informal settlements are burgeoning in the countryside and around the cities, farmers and suburbanites alike are arming themselves to the teeth. Daily reports of robbery and murder and the widespread possession of AK47s and stolen firearms by the poor only add to the fears of the rich old millions. They build defences around their houses using the latest electronic surveillance devices, they move their businesses out of the central business districts to the suburbs and they have guards to keep the highways to the airports open.

The purchase of a gun may be regarded as a rational reaction to the threats around us, but it merely ratchets up the potential for violence. Certainly it is a myth to believe that it can lead in the long run to the kind of society which we wish to bequeath to our children.

The alternative is not charity but constructive engagement. Recently, I challenged a business audience in Cape Town to think not only about taking the next plane overseas to clinch another deal in London but also about seeking to place contracts with the informal sector in any of the numerous townships ringing the city. Although the immediate financial rewards of the latter initiative might bear no resemblance to the former, ultimately it might mean more in terms of survival.

An intriguing question to ask about the future South Africa is what her attitude towards her neighbours will be in the event of her becoming the first African tiger. Will she erect high walls on her borders to ensure that she does not become the sump for all displaced persons in the region? Or will she create a Southern African Common Market which spreads sufficient new wealth around to create a stable and prosperous subcontinent? The answer, as the song says, is "blowing in the wind".

The end of the cold war has made the world more stable

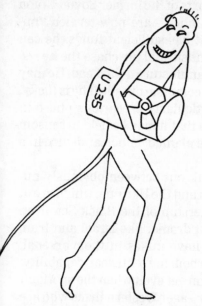

Not a bit of it! It has thrown the world into confusion. The previous American president, George Bush, talked of the New World Order. What we in fact have is the New World Disorder. The Cold War had two stabilising features. Firstly, most countries were clients of one or other superpower. If any of them stepped out of line and became a potential threat to world peace, its ambition was quickly subdued by the respective superpower. Secondly, the former Soviet Union had cohesion in its nuclear strike capability. Neither of these features is present any more because of the weakness of the structures that have replaced the Soviet Union.

The United States is not willing to play global cop if the going is too tough. Nor is Europe or Japan inclined to back her up if military force is required. The United Nations is making a brave attempt to act as fire fighter in the world's trouble spots, but its budgets and resources are dangerously overstretched. A vacuum now exists which some dangerous power-crazy despot could easily exploit.

Nevertheless, the second uncertainty concerning nuclear weapons is far more alarming. Parts of the former Soviet Union – particularly the southern republics – are now termed "nuclear bazaars". Provided a client has sufficient funds, he can recruit out-of-work nuclear scientists and purchase the necessary uranium or plutonium to manufacture a warhead. He may even be able to lay his hands on a complete missile if he is lucky. The world is moving into a particularly precarious phase in which it is not out of the question that it may be held to ransom by a group of terrorists who have planted a nuclear device in a major Western city.

Alternatively, a war may break out between obviously nuclear-armed rivals such as Russia and the Ukraine, which are at present scrapping over the ownership of the Black Sea fleet. Major players in the Middle East drama, like Israel and Iran, may suddenly reveal that they have nukes in their arsenal. North Korea may be secretly harbouring a nuclear capability: Iraq demonstrated how far you can get even when the spotlight is on you. There appear to be ever-eager Western firms who are prepared to supply equipment that can be converted into making the Bomb, but who resolutely maintain their innocence if the deal is discovered. Their excuses are that the client assured them of the peaceful use of the components supplied, and that they were unaware that the client was obtaining other vital parts elsewhere.

The only way that these scenarios can be pre-empted is by ultra-strict arms control imposed by the United Nations. In particular, the International Atomic Energy Agency must be beefed up to fulfil its role of inspecting the facilities of countries with nuclear capability and of checking the international trade in nuclear materials. Moreover, greater sanctions will have to be applied both to nations which have signed the Nuclear Nonproliferation Treaty but are not abiding by its terms of inspection, and to nations which are still nonsignatories but are known to conduct nuclear research. The same conditions should also apply to the poor man's options of biological and chemical weapons. The rich nations will also have to fork out considerably more funds for the conventional forces which the United Nations are currently deploying around the world. Otherwise, that institution will go bust.

It's all about the brotherhood of man, man

In the 1960s, teenagers all sang the words of the hit tune "If you're going to San Francisco, be sure to wear some flowers in your hair . . ." and they really meant it. The flowers were the Hippie symbol of universal love and peace. Maybe they were naive to have such ideals of international brotherhood in those days, but the world since then has turned out to be the exact opposite.

The last few years have seen fragmentation of peoples on a scale which few if any professional futurists were predicting even as late as the mid 1980s. An empire, namely the Soviet Union, has broken up relatively peacefully, although age-old antagonisms have been reignited in the southern regions. Czechoslovakia has also experienced a velvet divorce. However, Yugoslavia has been shattered by the most brutal of civil wars. In Africa, strife between rival clans still abounds. This all goes to show that nationalism, language and culture are very powerful life forces.

In order to overcome these forces, one must create powerful overarching loyalties. The Americans have just about managed to do this, notwithstanding the current polarisation in many of their communities. The yardstick by which one measures the degree to which clannishness has been overcome is to ask an individual where he is from. More often than not, an American will reply "from the United States". In contrast, if you ask a Scot, a Welshman or an Englishman his country of origin, you will seldom get the reply "Britain". Somehow, the Kingdom has never been that United in the eyes of its various tribes.

The message for South Africa from the recent phenomenon of fragmentation is that the Grail of brotherhood across lines of race and ethnicity, however earnestly sought, is extremely hard to find. Certainly, a piece of paper like a new constitution – even if it is carefully crafted by the slickest lawyers in town – is not going to hold clans together. The best glue will be if South Africa turns out to be the powerhouse of the African continent, an example for the rest of sub-Saharan Africa to follow. Success is the key. Everyone wants to belong to a successful club.

Today, one of the major obstacles to creating cross-cultural ties is the sheer size of nations, cities, companies and other institutions where people are brought together. Kinship, companionship and human contact are lost. One therefore has to look to smaller entities – like villages, company plants and sports teams – to find these qualities. The finest example that I can quote is the South African gold-mining industry, a polyglot community if ever there was one. The low gold price in the last few years and the threat of mine closures served to fuse the miners on every shaft into highly effective and cooperative teams. Over and above the economic situation, the special dangers of mining deep in the bowels of the earth generate a feeling of camaraderie that exists in no other business. Underground, there is no such thing as colour.

Hand-outs work

This myth was particularly prevalent in the 1970s and 1980s when huge amounts of international aid were distributed to developing countries. However, in view of the many failures associated with these hand-outs, august bodies like the IMF and the World Bank have revised their views.

Straight hand-outs don't work for several reasons. Probably the most important objection is that frequently only a small fraction of the original donation arrives in the hands of the intended recipient. There is plenty of "line loss" on the way, including the salaries of the bureaucrats employed in the distribution chain (an honest absorption), the siphoning off of large sums by government officials in the recipient countries (a dishonest absorption) and difficult local conditions such as a civil war, lack of transport and a poor communication network. A second objection is that hand-outs create a dependency culture which can utterly undermine the will of people to do anything for themselves and destroy any free enterprise system that already exists in the community. A third objection is that much of the aid has been misdirected into grandiose projects that have turned into miserable white elephants or, worse still, destroyed the environment.

A subsidiary myth under this heading is that affirmative action works when it is a crude disguise for handing out jobs to a favoured group. Not only does this cut across the natural wish for justice and meritocracy in society (can you imagine how school children would react if they felt that their teacher was giving extra marks in a completely arbitrary way to favourites?), but it also leads to tokenism which lumps together competent and incompetent members of the favoured group, satisfying nobody. However, there is an essential place for affirmative action in education and training to provide equality of opportunity in the workplace, as opposed to equality of outcome.

Another subsidiary myth concerns the value of governmental welfare and entitlement programmes. It is now common cause in America that workfare should replace welfare, i.e. that needy and disadvantaged people should, wherever possible, be given skills rather than money so that they can stand up for themselves, support their families and feel a sense of fulfilment and achievement in doing so. The problem is that hand-outs degrade the people receiving them. They never give hope.

In South Africa, the most potent illustration of this myth is the almost unimaginable amounts of money that have been squandered in hand-outs to the homelands. If one wants strong, effective regional government, then it is a vital condition that much of the money to finance that government is raised locally. Only then the local taxpayers will have the motivation to hold their regional leaders accountable for every cent that is spent.

A high population growth is no problem

This myth is put forward by certain contrarian economists who believe that fast-growing populations are good for the market (more young people mean more consumption) and by some environmentalists who prefer to avoid linking any ecological problem to the poor. However, far more dangerous is that this myth is believed on the one hand by quite a few political leaders of developing countries who regard a large population as a symbol of a mighty nation, and on the other by the poor themselves who feel that any argument in favour of lowering birth rates is a rich man's ploy to undermine their one source of political strength and their one source of wealth in their old age – their numbers and their children respectively.

Nevertheless, the population figures speak for themselves. The world is now adding an extra one hundred million people every year to its population and South Africa one million. To put these numbers in perspective, the first one is equivalent to an additional America every two and a half years and the second means another complete South African population by 2030 (on the assumption that the annual increment doesn't climb as the population increases).

Mark Twain once said: "Buy land. They're not making it any more." The population pressure on land around the globe is growing to the extent that the arable land is shrinking as it becomes exhausted. This increases the pressure even more.

Only 13,5 per cent of South Africa is categorised as arable land, i.e. land on which one can grow crops without irrigation because the rainfall is sufficient. Already, parts of that arable land are extremely overpopulated. Furthermore, a water shortage is developing. Although schemes like the Lesotho Highlands Water project should see us through to the end of the century, in the next century water shortages will become critical. Can you imagine the risks of doubling the South African population under such circumstances, particularly when our weather conditions are so erratic?

The most effective means to curb population growth are fourfold: a general rise in income per head; an improvement in educational standards; an enhancement in the status of women; and an effective network of family planning clinics.

The one wild card which could stop our population doubling so quickly is Aids. Nevertheless, anybody who says that Aids is a blessing for this reason is crazy. The extent of human tragedy, the economic blow to industry, the astronomical rise in health costs and the plague mentality which will ensue in the event of an Aids epidemic are things one would wish on no nation.

Economic development matters more/less than the environment

Either way, a categoric statement of this sort is a myth. The balance between economic and environmental priorities depends on the circumstances of each case. One has to weigh the economic benefits of any project against the potential environmental degradation. This is not as simple as it sounds because, in essence, one is comparing apples with pears. It is very hard, if not impossible, to put a monetary value on environmental loss. Hence, the tendency is for debates between business and green lobbies to deteriorate into slanging matches, the former caricaturing the latter as an impractical bunch of Mother Earthers dressed up in smocks and the latter likening the former to ruthless, cigar-smoking capitalists decked out in pinstripes.

In short, no hard rules apply, no blueprints are available. Whether it is constructing another coal-burning power station in the Highveld, cattle ranching in the Okavango, or mining sand dunes at St Lucia, kaolin on Chapman's Peak or coal in the Kruger Park – to take the most emotive examples – it all comes down to a matter of good judgement. In these cases, other than the power station, one can put economic arguments on the table for not going ahead in that a major tourist attraction could be destroyed. A less obvious, but no less controversial issue in some quarters, is the planting of exogenous forests in the Eastern Transvaal and Natal. "Green cancer," exclaim the naturalists. "Jobs and foreign exchange," reply the businessmen. Somehow a balance has to be struck between the two opposing viewpoints, namely that some land but not all of the land should be planted with trees.

Governments can tilt the playing field in favour of the environment in several ways. Firstly, there can be outright prohibition of certain activities such as the dumping of toxic waste in ecologically sensitive areas – with large fines if such bans are flouted. Secondly, through taxes and fiscal incentives, businesses can be steered along environmentally friendly paths. Thirdly, the environment can be made a core subject on school curricula so that over time an environmental ethic spreads throughout society. Having said this, the worst thing that can happen is for the environment to be used as an excuse for excessive government intervention in the economy.

Regarding global problems like the depletion of the ozone layer and the possibility that the burning of fossil fuels is linked to the greenhouse effect, humanity will have to review its "culture of more" – more cars, more television sets, more material goods generally. But who is going to tell China, or any other developing country for that matter, that they cannot have as much as the rich nations currently have because the rules have changed? Who is going to act as Big Brother in defining the limits of consumption for each individual consumer – two cars or one? And remember: "less" could mean more unemployment.

Socialism works

Give one example. Even the much vaunted Swedish "Third Way" has been abandoned by the Swedes themselves, because the high level of tax which had to be paid for the high level of welfare was suffocating the economy.

As for the argument that the Far East has a benign form of government intervention and is therefore a fine example of socialism at work, this is mental gymnastics at its worst. Nowhere will you find a more wholehearted acceptance of capitalism than among the ordinary Taiwanese, South Koreans, Thais, Singaporeans, etc. Even the Chinese in the coastal provinces of China have demonstrated how totally switched on to the profit motive they are. You will witness on any street corner in any Far Eastern city entrepreneurs selling their goods and services all day and all night. They don't even think for one second of state assistance. They know that it is their own hard work and commitment that will lead to some prosperity for themselves and their families.

Yes, there is government intervention in the Asian tigers, but it is purely on the basis of encouraging and ensuring that business is successful in local and foreign markets. This is light years away from the socialist attitude that money is the root of all evil and that the profit motive should be exorcised from society. Moreover, the role that government plays in these economies is one of coach to the team rather than chief executive of the commanding heights of the economy. However, when all is said and done, the statistic that clinches the difference between Far Eastern governments and those with socialist inclinations is the percentage that government expenditure represents of total GNP. The figure runs at around 20 per cent in places like Thailand and Singapore, whereas in socialist economies one is looking at 50 per cent or more.

Socialism fails precisely because it does not understand, or accept, that man is basically competitive by nature and will produce his best results by pursuing his own self-interest in a competitive environment. It also fails because of the vanity of intellectuals who believe that they can orchestrate the millions of decisions which are made every day in a complex economy.

Yet socialism has left its mark on modern society. Aspects like trade unionism and the welfare state, which many socialists fought for in the last century and at the beginning of this one, are now considered perfectly legitimate by anyone with reasonable political views. Indeed, they are now part and parcel of the free enterprise system.

The world is run by twelve bankers

In this myth, the twelve bankers usually come from famous, extremely wealthy families, many of whom are Jewish. They meet monthly in New York to plot the movements of capital around the world, deciding which countries to back and which countries to pull the plug on. They give their blessing to presidents, prime ministers and leaders of all kinds before they can stand for office. They orchestrate global booms and depressions, stock market rises and falls. They manipulate currencies and determine the direction of the gold and bond markets. They even start wars and stop them. It is extraordinary how widely this story, which is sometimes referred to as "the conspiracy theory", is believed. Many books have been written on it, which are nothing more than right-wing mumbo jumbo. The popularity of the theory probably rests on the fact that two powerful themes have been merged – anti-Semitism and anti-big business.

While no evidence exists to suggest that any such meetings ever took place, theoretically they could have been possible in the first fifty years of this century, because of the immense power of American and European business. However, economic power is now more widely dispersed in the world, having particularly moved to the Far East. From now on, therefore, no twelve tycoons of whatever nationality will ever be able to wield collectively the level of influence on world affairs that the myth implies.

Occasionally, an individual does have an impact on world markets. The name crops up again and again for a time. "Mr So-and-So has just moved out of dollars into gold," the headlines scream. The dollar weakens, gold strengthens and you feel that this man really does have colossal power. Normally, though, the markets eventually catch out anyone involved in big-time speculation. One wrong move, the magic fades and the world moves on to another oracle.

The press should be neutral

The press is never neutral. It's a myth to try and make it so. Each newspaper, each radio station and each television channel is vying for the maximum possible audience. They have a rough idea about the opinions of their readers, listeners and viewers and will inevitably frame the facts in different ways by using different adjectives, emphases and omissions to please their respective audiences. We always complain in South Africa that the overseas press only writes bad news. But bad news travels fast and good news is often no news.

Two stories illustrate my point. I asked an American correspondent of a weekly news magazine what he looked for in the copy that he submitted to his editors back home. He bluntly replied that whites killing whites and blacks killing blacks were hardly news in America. However, blacks killing whites and whites killing blacks immediately received serious coverage. In his case, therefore, any story on violence was screened through an important "popularity" filter before it was sent.

The second example concerns a British television producer who came to South Africa in 1988 on a short trip to make a definitive documentary on the country. In a conversation at a dinner party in Pretoria, before the shoot, he stoutly maintained to the assembled guests that he was going to be thoroughly objective. In the next breath, he paid glowing tribute to his mother who had never bought an unmarked orange in any supermarket in England for fear of its being from South Africa. For all his television savvy, he was totally unconscious of the apparent contradiction between these two statements to a South African audience.

I am in no way suggesting that the media should change its approach. *The Guardian* will always tell it differently from *The Daily Telegraph* and *The Weekly Mail* from *The Citizen*. They appeal to different markets. But if one acknowledges the bias of the media, the most effective way in which society can get at the truth on any issue is by having as many sources as possible. This means that South Africa should have as many independently owned newspapers and magazines as the market can bear, and as many independent television channels and radio stations as the airwaves permit. Any controversy in 1993 surrounding the composition of the SABC Board would not have occurred if the Corporation was privatised and competed against one or two other national networks; in other words, if we followed the American route of having rival television stations and possibly a public service channel as well.

One of the nicest quotations I have come across about how one should be circumspect on what the press says came from a noted member of the left-wing British intelligentsia. He said: "Don't always believe what the press said you said. You may have changed your mind."

The press needs a watchdog

A myth related to the previous one is that a new government should install a watchdog over the press. Proponents of this idea say it is the only way to ensure that the press is reasonable and responsible. The problem is that "reasonable and responsible" means different things to different people, the common thread being flattering to one's own views and critical of one's opponents'. The best way to achieve a balance between freedom of expression and reasonableness is to have sensible laws on libel and pornography, and recourse to the courts. This implies an independent judiciary.

Interestingly, in Britain of all places, the recent negative coverage of the Royal Family has elicited calls for a tougher body to oversee media propriety. Yet even panels set up by the press themselves to discipline individual members who stray from the industry's consensus of acceptability can be dangerous. If the definition of inflammatory language is too broad, it becomes a means of censorship.

One must not underestimate the public. If a particular newspaper or television station gains a reputation for lies and calumny, people will simply stop buying the newspaper or watching the channel. They'll see through the propaganda and move to another source of news. The advertisers will drift away and the newspaper or television station will go into liquidation. Much better that the market closes the institution down than an official or semi-official watchdog!

Aids is a Western plot

This ultra-dangerous myth circulates among disadvantaged communities in Africa. For many, Aids means "American invention to discourage sex". This myth is one of the reasons why so many well-intentioned programmes to educate the masses about the dangers of Aids have failed. Among other reasons, of course, are that the Aids virus is invisible and that it lies dormant for so many years. One therefore has to be extremely careful in choosing the medium and the message so that neither is tinged with condescension or racism.

Probably the most effective method to date here has been the use of theatre and puppets to dramatise the consequences of promiscuousness. However, until community leaders openly and outspokenly lend their credibility to Aids awareness programmes, this myth will continue.

The fact is that unless we do something now in South Africa to change the potential spread of Aids, we could end up with four million HIV positive cases in the year 2000, or some 8 per cent of our population. The window of opportunity to stop Aids turning into an epidemic here is very short, with a doubling time for HIV cases estimated at twelve months. For the world as a whole the HIV estimate for the year 2000 ranges between a figure of 40 and 100 million. This means that South Africa could have between 4 and 10 per cent of the world's cases, while having only 0,8 per cent of the world's population. We shall suffer more than most.

All liberals are soft

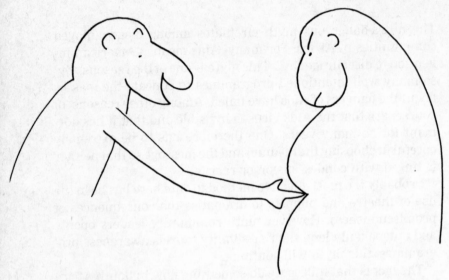

For many years in South Africa, this myth has been widely upheld – particularly in conservative circles. The term "liberal" has been used to denote someone who falls just short of being a communist. Perhaps the only perceived difference between the two was that a communist was hard and lethal whereas a liberal was soft and ever-willing to make concessions to the demands of the majority.

The reality is that liberalism in the world at large has evolved from the "hard" classical version which laid maximum stress on individual liberty and freedom of speech to an almost contrary "soft" philosophy which in its modern form is personified by the American Democratic Party. This philosophy, by contrast, favours government intervention in order to bring about a more egalitarian, just and caring society. Franklin Roosevelt's "New Deal" to offset the ravages of the Depression during the 1930s is considered a perfect example of the later form of liberalism at work.

Here in South Africa we have both types of liberal, the "soft" version now being close to a social democrat. Nevertheless, the torch of "hard" liberalism has been carried by some outstanding individuals such as Helen Suzman and Ken Owen. Given the predilection of some of the principal political players for big government, "hard" liberals have never had a more vital role to play than in persuading the powers that be, or to be, of the necessity for minimising governmental interference in the lives of ordinary people.

Talk is progress

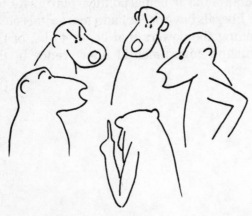

This myth has some validity to it in that if there is no "jaw-jaw" there is likely to be "war-war". So, may all the forums for negotiation and development of future policies continue. Nevertheless, South Africa has to have the highest number of conferences, workshops and commissions of inquiry per head of the population in any country in the world. Moreover, given the size of conference fees, one can't even say that talk is cheap!

We have this vast world of talk and good intentions and a minuscule world of action: somehow, we have to convert more of the one into the other. As the saying goes, action speaks louder than words. One of the prime causes for paralysis beyond the talking stage is another myth: that somebody somewhere must be asked for permission. After all, "rules and regulations" need to be observed. Until the form has been filled in and the "red tape" has been gone through, nobody must do anything.

This helplessness is a direct descendant of South Africa's centrist tradition which elsewhere I have called "Pretoria will provide". Until people break free of that tradition and honestly believe that, when they come out of that conference hall, they as individuals can really make a difference to their local communities without having to wait for anybody's say-so, nothing will happen. This isn't a call for revolution and anarchy, both of which tend to be destructive. However, this is a call to replace the top-down approach that has slowed down virtually every creative activity in this country to a snail's pace with spontaneous action from the grass roots. Old habits die hard, but die they must.

It's all your fault

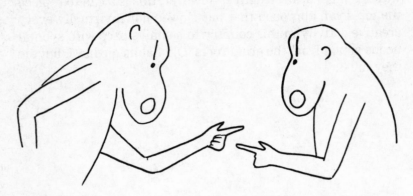

A sad legacy of the divided society that we have had in South Africa for so many years is that the concept of being held responsible for one's own actions has been eroded to virtual non-existence. The four magic words "it's all my fault" do not pass South African lips. It is always your fault. Everyone points fingers at everyone else, and when there is no one to point fingers at, the "system" takes the rap or a shadowy "third force" is assigned the blame.

With the dwindling in personal responsibility, individuals surrender their self-restraint to the frenzy of the crowd. The lives of the "enemy" – often innocent bystanders – are devalued to the point where it seems only natural that they should be lynched. Justice is instant and another human being is snuffed out. We now have random and senseless drive-by shootings. We hardly listen to the weekend news when it starts with "Four men with AK47s in a green car opened fire on people standing in a taxi rank. Five were killed and seven were injured. The car, which had been stolen, was later found abandoned . . ." Husbands shooting their families and then themselves, motorists slain when they break down on the highway – these actions are symptoms of a total breakdown in accountability.

The fundamental condition for a viable society is that each individual is held fully accountable for his or her actions. The law has to be upheld and be seen to be upheld. Moreover, until leaders stand up in public and accept the blame for the wayward actions of their followers with a commitment to bring them into line, we will not even begin to make progress in lowering the equilibrium of violence.

I can do no better than quote John Donne, the 17th century metaphysical poet, who wrote: "Any man's death diminishes me, because I am involved in Mankind; and therefore never send to know for whom the bell tolls; it tolls for thee."

"It's all your fault" is an evil myth. We shall all be to blame if this country descends into chaos.

You are all going to leave as penniless refugees

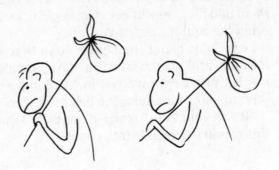

When South African émigrés return to these shores on a trip to see their friends and relatives, it is an opportunity to listen to some hilarious exchanges because of the hidden agendas on both sides. The émigrés secretly wish to justify their decision to leave in the first place. They therefore eulogise their new home, saying how wonderful it is to be able to go out without locking the doors of the house and to discuss anything but politics at dinner parties. Meanwhile, they still paint only one apocalyptic scenario for this country, viz. that South Africa will soon be engulfed in civil war and turned into a wasteland. Normally, they put a time limit of eighteen months on this scenario. Yet South Africa defies a time limit. So, to their intense surprise, normal life goes on and the country, like a block of well-weathered granite, remains intact. This makes them homesick. All they can do, therefore, is earnestly hope that one day events will prove that their decision was the right one.

By contrast, the friends and relatives still here tend to err on the bright side and say that no matter how bad it may seem, the quality of life here is better than anywhere else. These discussions can end up quite painfully and disagreeably, particularly if a few bottles of choice South African wine are imbibed to lubricate the conversation.

Naturally, as one still here, I favour the story of hope for this country and tend to find such émigrés and the myths they peddle for their own sakes fairly distasteful. As my favourite hymn says: "Whoso beset him round with dismal stories, do but themselves confound; his strength the more is . . ." That fairly represents the spirit of the people who stay.

Steady as she goes

Staying with the subject of emigration, here is a widely held Australian myth. Australia is pictured as a comfortable yacht sailing on calm seas. Any squalls that occur are well over the horizon. The crew has only two minor anxieties. Firstly, they appear to be on a never-ending cruise with no particular place to go. Secondly, when they return to port for provisions and repairs to the yacht, a strong rumour goes around that the owner is paying for these on credit because he has a minor overdraft of 168 billion Australian dollars (the nation's current foreign debt). Still, the owner doesn't seem too concerned so the crew aren't too anxious either. They set sail again and it's steady as she goes. By the way, the name of the yacht is *Lucky Country*.

The reason that this story is so popular in Australia is that the country has no perceived threat. But remember the story about the frog. If you put a frog into a saucepan of water that is gently heating up, the frog will die because it won't detect the incremental changes of temperature. If you dump a frog into boiling water, it will immediately rescue itself by jumping out.

The moral of this myth for South Africans is that at least here the downside scenarios for the country are well understood and publicised. We are on our guard to prevent them from materialising. In Matilda's case, someone has to tell her to stop waltzing in an unconcerned way and to step onto the modern ballroom floor with all the other Asian tigers. She needs to learn a new dance. Otherwise the appropriate title of Australia's future will be *On Golden Pond* – if you remember that marvellous movie with Katharine Hepburn and Henry Fonda which depicted an elderly couple descending imperceptibly into their autumn years. The one difference, of course, is that Katharine and Henry were not so heavily in debt. The grass isn't always greener on the other side!

Money will roll in as soon as we have achieved a settlement

Despite the tougher attitudes being exhibited overseas by banks and other financial institutions in the matter of loans and aid to developing countries, many South Africans are caught in a time warp. They firmly believe that the world owes them a living, provided the condition of becoming an acceptable democratic state is fulfilled. Zimbabwe demonstrated otherwise. Promises of billions of dollars from overseas sources after independence never materialised.

Western banks are fed up with making loans, the repayment of which has to be rescheduled and rescheduled because the borrower has turned into an economic basket case. They now thoroughly check out the credit ratings of their prospective clients beforehand. Aid agencies are no longer prepared to see their grants swallowed up into the Swiss bank accounts of corrupt officials of recipient governments. They now give money directly to projects. Nor do they wish to be associated with regimes that imprison, torture and kill their political opponents. This has elicited howls of protest from dictators who feel the sovereignty of their countries is being infringed by the imposition of such harsh conditions for aid.

South Africa at the moment is underborrowed and has a commendable record of repaying its loans, although certain extensions and roll-overs have been necessary. It might be possible for a newly elected democratic government here to embark on a borrowing binge which for a time would seem to confirm the myth that money is easily available. But the chickens would soon come home to roost and our hard-earned reputation which has taken a long time to establish with international bankers would be irreversibly tarnished.

As far as foreign investment is concerned, we also have a magnificent chance of attracting the top world-class companies to put money into projects here. After all, we have the best infrastructure in Africa in terms of roads, railways, telecommunications, electricity grid and airports. We also possess a fully fledged tax code and system of commercial law. However, a remarkable video produced by the South African Chamber of Commerce, in which a potential investor in a series of slides compares the relative merits of investing in South Africa with those in other countries, clearly indicates how incredibly stiff the competition is in terms of tax holidays, investment allowances, low unit wage costs and other measures of economic efficiency.

South Africa needs to realise that the formula for a winning nation is spreading fast around the world, giving international companies many more options in terms of developing global business networks. Any future government must therefore behave as an eager matchmaker, wooing the hard-nosed managers that make the investment decisions overseas to consider us as eligible material. Any sign of arrogance will condemn us to eternal spinsterhood.

Big business is too big for its boots

Over the past five years, a campaign has been waged to prove that big business, and in particular the four or five largest groups, have a disproportionate amount of economic power in South Africa. Statistics are bandied about that the top five own some 80 per cent of the Johannesburg Stock Exchange. This equates in people's minds to ownership of the economy as a whole. Not only is the estimate per se of 80 per cent for the big five's ownership of JSE shares exaggerated, but the fact that large parts of the economy are in the hands of the state and of businesses not quoted on the JSE is conveniently forgotten.

Perhaps the best measure of the relative size of the major actors in the South African economy is the percentage of GDP that they contribute. For the top five businesses together, the total is probably in the range of 15 to 20 per cent of GDP. This compares with government expenditure which is 35 per cent of GDP. Stealing the image of the octopus, the one which opponents of big business (wrongly) use to portray it, any sane person will come to the conclusion that the octopus with the longest tentacles by far is government!

Relative to giants overseas against which domestic companies compete in many fields internationally, South African big business is actually modestly sized. For example, the combined market capitalisation of the top ten companies in South Africa is less than that of the single largest American company, Exxon. Nevertheless, South Africa is one of the few developing countries to have world-class companies to undertake large projects at home and overseas, to earn critical foreign currency and to attract top-rate foreign partners for joint ventures. It is preposterous that South African business should be condemned purely for its size. Instead, it should be judged on the kind of performance parameters that apply to any large company anywhere in the world. The usual criteria include its growth in earnings and dividends, the capital appreciation of its shares over time, its innovative products and new projects, its conditions of employment and its social contribution to the community. Taking the last twenty years as a base of suitable longevity, the best of the big companies here would come out of an international comparison pretty well.

The last paragraph also exposes an associated myth – South African companies are monopolies. This term is loosely used to imply that companies here unscrupulously corner the market to raise the price of their product or service to whatever level they like, because no other supplier is around. Firstly, most South African companies are in competition either with other local producers in the same field or with international concerns. They are fighting for market share and have little influence over either price (gold, copper and other commodities) or demand (cars, household appliances).

Secondly, where a South African company dominates the market, such as South African Breweries does in the case of the beer market, the principal reason is that economies of scale and the efficiencies associated with using the latest state-of-the-art technologies allow the company to lower its price to a level which few, if any others, can match. That's hardly the monopolistic practice of price-gouging!

It would be a tragedy if a future competition board broke up a large company on ideological grounds and the result was higher prices and lower quality to customers from its smaller offspring. Should additional competition in a particular sector of the domestic economy be considered a must, the best ways to go about achieving that goal are to eradicate any tariff barriers on imports into that market and to attract international producers to set up shop here.

Capitalism and apartheid go hand in hand

It's a sad myth: many people who suffered under apartheid believe that capitalism and apartheid are handmaidens. Yet capitalism too suffered under apartheid because the latter placed major restrictions on entrepreneurship, on free enterprise and on the movement of people, capital and goods to where the markets demanded they should go. An ideology was placed above the natural laws of economics and proved very costly in human and material terms.

One cannot deny what history reveals. Some unscrupulous businessmen used apartheid as a tool to further their own goals. But businessmen, like socialists and others, come in the good, the bad and the ugly variety. There are plenty of capitalists who care. One can cite many examples of businessmen boldly speaking out against apartheid, funding initiatives against its most pernicious consequences, and beginning the process of reconciliation (remember the famous visit to Lusaka by businessmen to meet the ANC).

It is said that "corporations have neither bodies to be punished nor souls to be damned". However, they have shareholders to whom they are accountable. More and more of those shareholders are asking questions about the ethical track record of the corporations in which they have invested. Special funds have been created which are only invested in socially aware companies. In fact, the proportion of profits that many large businesses in South Africa divert into social responsibility programmes is well above the figure in the US and UK.

The truth is that capitalism and apartheid have nothing in common. The only colour that capitalism recognises is green – the colour of money!

Money brings you happiness

Having ended on such a materialistic note in disposing of the previous myth, I feel that the next one I should tackle is "Money brings you happiness". The negative statement is certainly true: no money brings you unhappiness. Moreover, the happiness curve rises steeply from zero income to a level where the necessities of life can be comfortably paid for. Thereafter, happiness and income levels become increasingly independent of one another. In other words, there are some modestly well-off people who are extremely happy and some mega-rich people who are totally miserable (and vice versa). Occasionally, of course, there are the saintly exceptions who do not have two brass farthings to rub together but who have reached an exceptional plane of happiness through helping others.

It is interesting to note that values in the rich nations in the 1990s have swung away from self-indulgence and gross consumerism to health and quality of life. Hedonism is out and the search for an authentic meaning to life is in. Religious movements everywhere are expanding their numbers because of the emphasis being laid by the young on spiritual values. They are rejecting the materialistic ambitions of their parents because they feel that these values are responsible for the present sorry mess of the world (see the first myth – "Mankind has become more civilised").

Perhaps there's a divine hand in the paradox that the more successful you become in worldly terms, the more prone to anxieties and fears you are. For many successful people, in retrospect, the state of travelling hopefully towards the achievement of one's ambitions brings a great deal more pleasure than the arrival. Anyway, let's face it, life would be far less exciting and even more unfair if material and spiritual rewards were closely correlated.

A national minimum wage is a good thing

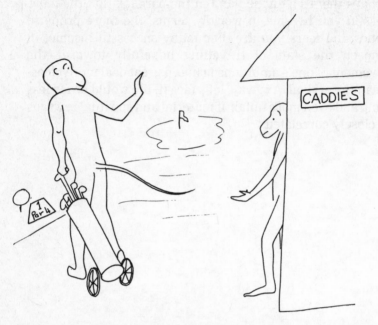

If you accept the theory put forward in the previous myth, that the happiness curve is steepest from zero to modest income levels, then the most beneficial way you can increase the sum total of a nation's happiness is to focus on the zero-income earners, i.e. the unemployed, and create an environment in which they can find jobs. The number of jobs, therefore, is more important than the level of wages. Moreover, a national minimum wage which destroys job opportunities is massively counterproductive for society.

Let me give a highly specific illustration which involves the use of caddies at a Johannesburg golf club. In the 1970s, virtually all members used a caddy because there was no minimum caddy fee. The market rationally allocated the caddies to the players, the best ones volunteering their services to the highest paying members and the least experienced going to the lowest paying ones.

Then the club decided that it was morally indefensible to pay below a certain amount per round, so minimum caddy fees were instituted. The net result was that a large number of members, particularly the elderly ones on fixed pensions, opted to push their own carts. Consequently, the number of caddies used has decreased dramatically. The club in effect has created two classes of caddies: a small class of caddies who are paid well and a large class of caddies who no longer have jobs. You can bet that the collective misery generated among the latter totally outweighs the additional happiness of the former. Thus, the club has achieved the diametrically opposite result of what it set out to do.

This is a cautionary tale for all would-be social engineers. Don't interfere in the way wages are set in any industry, whether they are formally determined through company-union negotiations (the two parties have a better idea than outsiders about what the economic conditions of the industry can afford), or whether they are informally fixed on a deal-by-deal basis as is normal in the small business and service sectors.

The road to hell is paved with good intentions.

I'm sorry I'm late

This apology is offered too often in South Africa for it not to be a convenient lie, which therefore qualifies it as a myth. However, it's not like other convenient lies such as "we must have lunch some time", which is a polite way of putting off a meeting into the indefinite future. This one really hurts the functioning of society, where punctuality is the soul of business and time is money. The audiences, the visitors and the public who are on the receiving end of this thoughtless and arrogant type of behaviour – after all the person keeping others waiting obviously feels his time is more important than theirs – have come to shrug their shoulders, and let it be.

The best method of instilling a sense of punctuality in VIPs is to follow the American example of publishing an annual list of the "worst" in various categories. Whereas the Americans go for the "worst dressed", we would have, among others, "worst for turning up for meetings on time", "worst at double-dating", "worst for not returning phone calls" and so on. Nobody likes to have his shortcomings pointed out in public, even in such a good-humoured way.

Big is safe

This myth has been around a long time. The passengers who happily boarded the *Titanic* in 1912 believed in it. Latterly, the investors in some blue-chip American, European and Japanese companies have discovered the myth to their great cost. Instinctively we prefer big planes, big ships and big cars to travel in (the fellow who went over Chapman's Peak and survived was right!). Bankers prefer lending money to big companies, sometimes in retrospect having thrown caution to the winds when the dazzling tycoon that beguiled them turns out to be an incompetent rogue.

Obviously, one should not go to the opposite extreme and reach the conclusion that everything that is big is risky. From Mercedes cars to Boeing 747s to many world-class companies, ample testimony exists that this is not so. So when is big safe?

The answer, as far as companies are concerned, lies in the attitude of management towards change. If management is complacent, never questions the mission statement of the company to see if it is still applicable to the market, and stubbornly feels that it can shape the future according to its own wishes, the red lights are beginning to flash. There is no such thing as "business as usual". Every week goes to show that business has become highly unusual! As a child I often worried about the well-known biblical statement: "Blessed are the meek, for they shall inherit the earth." It didn't seem to make sense to me at school, where the strong inherited everything. Now I've changed my mind. Those who meekly and humbly accept that the future is uncertain, and that unexpected opportunities and threats may force them swiftly to revise their opinions and judgements, usually win out in the end. To the nimble-minded go the spoils.

Ironically, one of the most sensible strategies to keep big business safe is to have a diversified portfolio of activities which is resilient under virtually any economic scenario. It's a case of not putting all your eggs into one basket. Yet the fashionable idea of "unbundling" does just that – separates the baskets so you have to choose which one to put your eggs in!

A good industrial relations agreement brings job security

This myth is allied to the previous one: "Big is safe". Go tell the millions who have been laid off from large companies in America, Europe and now Japan that they should put their faith in the agreements on job protection that their unions negotiated on their behalf. Nobody would dispute that there is scant value in having a code of conduct between a ship's captain and the crew if the ship is sinking. Likewise, little purpose is served in drafting the most detailed industrial relations agreement covering every aspect of conditions of employment and work environment if the company's market share is plummeting.

In a free market, you cannot compel customers to purchase your product. You cannot force them to pay a price for that product which will cover its costs and provide a reasonable profit to be reinvested in new plant, and give the shareholders a decent return. Hence, if those costs have been boosted by high wage escalation, generous fringe benefits and restrictive work practices to a level which the market rejects, then jobs will automatically be at risk. As the stocks of unsold goods increase, so the workforce will decline.

This all goes to show that a union which blindly pursues its mission of achieving the best conditions for its members can actually make its members pay the ultimate sacrifice – that of losing their jobs. The customers have moved on to alternative sources and they'll probably never come back.

Despite its transparent irrationality, this myth is responsible for assisting in the decline of many industries in the wealthy nations. The way to escape falling into the same trap is for companies to share the essential information needed for judging the viability and future prospects of the industry concerned with the union leaders. Above all, the belief that whatever a company produces can automatically be sold at any price must be buried for good.

Family values are uncool

This myth, like the "Brotherhood of Man" myth, dates back to the Swinging Sixties. Its origin lies in the rejection of the staid lifestyle of the 1950s and its replacement by long hair, mini-skirts and bell-bottomed trousers (harmless enough and short-lived) and by drugs, transient relationships and sexual promiscuity (nasty and long-lived). Unlike the "Brotherhood of Man" which is a perfectly reasonable, albeit unrealisable, goal, the myth about family values being uncool has therefore had devastating consequences for society.

Around one half of American marriages now end up in divorce. Whether or not marital vows are exchanged, millions of children are brought up in single-parent families, which means in effect by their mother because their father has left home. Worse still, the phenomenon of street children – children dumped by both their parents – is assuming frightening proportions. These children are easily enticed into prostitution, drug-running and other crimes. In some South American cities, they are brutally murdered whilst sleeping on the streets by vigilante groups wishing to stamp out crime.

Yet, pick up any glossy magazine you care to name and you are sure to find an article implying that a husband or wife who doesn't have lovers, or a wife who stays at home to rear her children and doesn't have a professional job, is an exceedingly boring person. Read any biography these days and it is *de rigueur* to spill the beans on the sexual peccadilloes (more often alleged than proven) of the great man or woman concerned. Watch most modern movies and the hero or heroine's marriage is either in trouble or has recently broken up – Hollywood, for sure, doesn't glamorise marriage. Even the phrase "family values" has been derided by the American media as one only used by beyond-the-pale conservatives. If that isn't all, the modern glorification of sex (the highest income earner in Britain is currently a man who owns a string of soft-porn magazines) has led to an equally offensive myth that "studs" are the "main dudes". Date rape is therefore replacing dating as a "legitimate" activity among young men.

Denigrating the family and putting the single swinger on a pedestal are very strange when one recalls that the place where a child receives the most love and affection, where a child learns values and self-discipline and where a child develops the personality and character and thereby the confidence to face the world, is the home. The family is the basic nucleus of society, as people in countries like India, China and Japan know. Without the familial web, society becomes a jungle in which no amount of laws and police can control the uncared-for and undisciplined youth.

To lead is to command

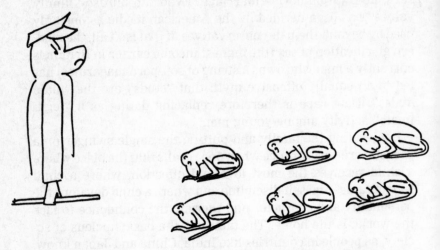

An unfortunate legacy of one's childhood is the belief that the only thing anybody of any importance ever does is issue instructions. Parents, teachers, prefects, army sergeants – they're all the same. Any sentence they utter starts with either "Do" or "Don't".

All these early experiences combine to give the impression that a good leader is a commander. In certain circumstances it is true. History is replete with wars and battles that were won by good commanders. But in politics and business the ability to command, to put one's foot down, to control one's followers, is merely one aspect of leadership. To think that one should run a country or a company by solely resorting to the heavy exercise of power is a myth. An equally important aspect of a leader is the ability to inspire other people to come out of their shells and fulfil their own potential, to challenge them to have ambitious dreams and then exceed those dreams.

Leadership is about empowering people to become leaders themselves by encouraging them to become better educated and trained. It's about giving your followers a sense of purpose, but then giving them the space to be creative within the framework of your vision. It's about having the common touch, so that the man and woman in the street, while respecting you, have the feeling that you're one of them and understand their hopes and fears. It's about putting forward new ideas yourself, but making people around you think that they thought of them first. It's about persuading doubters to your point of view and only at the last moment laying down the law if you can't. It's about occasionally saying no when everyone else wants you to say yes (and being proved correct!). It becomes statesmanship when you are gracious to your opponents in the broader interest.

Leadership comes in many forms. There is no one perfect style as those popular management textbooks suggest. The idea that you can take on somebody else's personality and habits and be a success with them is fraudulent. Be yourself, be natural and above all be consistent.

I would like to end this myth by quoting a senior Russian economist who was part of Gorbachev's team at the height of *glasnost*. She said that the biggest mistake that the Soviet Union made was to compel people to join collectives. In retrospect, she believed that the whole exercise should have been voluntary on the grounds that the goodwill of the Russian people would have led them to see the sense of communal solutions anyway. Whilst I still think she would have been wrong because she underestimated the attraction of private ownership of property and the power of the profit motive, she put her finger on the mighty myth of Marxism: to lead is to command.

Pretoria will provide

This is probably the most powerful myth to pervade South Africa. But South Africa is in good company. In Australia, it's Canberra that will provide, and in Canada it's Ottawa. The myth can be generalised to "The state will provide". Big government is a phenomenon of the 20th century. Income tax likewise.

At the beginning of this century, government expenditure in places like Europe and America was below 10 per cent of GNP. Now it ranges between 30 and 60 per cent of GNP. The citizens of these countries are taxed a great deal more than their 19th century counterparts, but a much higher proportion of them are now employed directly or indirectly by the state. Services like education and health are provided free, the indigent are on welfare, the unemployed are on the dole, farmers are given subsidies, the elderly receive pensions.

What is the net result? The world has created a new type of citizen, one whose instinctive reaction is to look to the state for the education of his children, for the health of his family, for monetary assistance in hard times, for employment as a last resort and for care in his old age. There's even a new word for all this assistance – entitlements. Having become dependent on these entitlements, this new citizen has come to regard the state as his saviour. He no longer fends for himself: communities no longer fend for themselves. Moreover, the opportunity for wasteful expenditure is staggering, because one has separated income (state taxes) from expenditure (state benefits) in the lives of most ordinary people. Firstly, many of the latter receive benefits when they are wealthy enough to do without them (middle-class Americans on welfare), and secondly, everybody spends their entitlements to the hilt because it's not their own money (the patient is not cost-conscious about health care). Over and above this, a massive bureaucracy has to administer

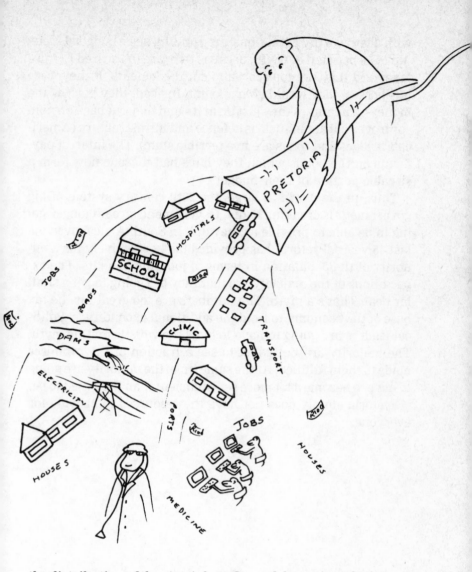

the distribution of the state's benefits and draws its salaries as a cost.

Governments around the world have created a most effective treadmill for themselves – citizens expecting more and more entitlements but at the same time citizens who are not prepared to pay higher taxes. Consequently, governments everywhere, with a few worthy exceptions, are running large budget deficits (up to 14 per cent of GNP), because they are too scared to raise taxes and they are too scared to cut the benefits. If they were businesses, they would go bankrupt. Instead, they borrow the money – sometimes they just print it – and they cut back on non-controversial areas such as defence and infrastructure (America's bridges and roads are in a terrible state). The interest payments on the bonds which they have had to issue now form a sizeable portion of their budget.

Thus, in the world at large, the 20th century system of big government is creaking badly. Governments are no longer going to be able to provide as they did. In South Africa, over the last 45 years, Pretoria has provided fairly effectively for a minority of the population in terms of jobs and benefits. The expectations of the majority are that they are going to get a similar deal. That's a myth. The numbers are too great for the tax base of the economy to fund the additional expenditure. Political leaders are going to have to blow the whistle on this myth. The majority are not going to see a fraction of the promises made to them fulfilled. At the same time, the minority are going to have to become a lot more self-sufficient than they used to be.

Pretoria simply does not have the resources to provide for everyone.

All "–"s are "–"

Pick any nationality for the first blank and any adjective, preferably one that is insulting, for the second blank. The tendency to generalise and thereby caricature other groups is present among all of us. For centuries the British have typecast the French as romantic and mercurial and vice versa as stiff and boring. Moreover, contrary to common belief, prejudice and educational achievement are independent of one another. In other words, highly educated people can be the most dreadful bigots.

A variation of the generalisation theme is the "heroes and villains" syndrome which crops up mainly in the press, where one side always comes up smelling of roses and the other of manure. We all know about this here! However, in South Africa's case, a far more serious issue has been the negative and simplistic stereotypes which each group possesses about the others through dearth of communication. It applies not only between groups divided by race and language, but also between different occupations – academia and business, government and business. You can picture South Africa as a collection of interlocking circles where there is tremendous communication inside each circle, but very little overlap or common ground as yet between them.

Misunderstandings and preconceptions frequently bedevil any debate when strangers from the different worlds fleetingly meet, usually in a television studio. The participants hardly ever see each other as free-thinking individuals trying to resolve problems and issues in a constructive manner, but as representatives of narrow sectional interests competing to propagate their views. I've always maintained that the only way to overcome the caricatures and stereotypes – which are invariably wrong because people on the whole are not that bad – is to sit the various sides down in a negotiating chamber day after day, night after night. One should lock the door of the room and throw away the key and then only let them out when, like the election of the Pope, white smoke issues from the chimney to indicate agreement.

Sheer human contact makes horns disappear. Thereafter, individuals begin to relate to each other as human beings, understanding each other's foibles and interests, hopes and fears.

There! I've made a lot of general statements in trying to address the problem of the myths that people have of one another. But, unlike the saying, not all generalisations in this piece are false!

Peasant farming can absorb the unemployed

It is a myth to believe that under a new political dispensation millions of poverty-stricken people can be settled on farming land expropriated by the state and make a go of subsistence farming. Because of low rainfall, the bulk of South Africa's land is simply not amenable to being broken up into small lots for crop production. Its only sustainable use is as pasture land, and even then the number of animals per hectare must be strictly limited. The last condition means that such land can only be exploited economically as large cattle or sheep ranches. As it is, the Karoo is dangerously overstocked with animals. The alternative is expensive irrigation schemes where the water has to be heavily subsidised. This is already creating water shortages for industrial and residential use, since half of South Africa's developed water resources is directed into irrigation.

Anyway, the concept of depositing masses of people on semi-arable land in rural areas remote from markets has been tried before. It was called the homeland policy. It has led to desertification, as every nook and cranny and slope is overintensively cultivated and overgrazed. It has caused deforestation as the women go on ever more distant forays for wood for their fires. And it has been responsible for acute shortages of drinking water where in some areas one tap serves more than 750 people. In Cambodia, Pol Pot, leaving to one side his programme of genocide, attempted the same approach of compulsory resettlement of peasants from urban to rural locations.

The fact is that the majority of South Africa's unemployed will have to be taught trades and small business skills and live in towns or villages. The pressure has to be taken off South Africa's land to stop further deterioration – not added to with millions of extra peasants. However, one brilliant conception was recently put forward by several agronomists – peri-urban market gardens using waste water. This is quite feasible because the market for vegetables, fruit and other products is close, roads and transport are available and the water would go to waste anyway. The sense in this proposal is that you start with the market and work back to the potential for creating jobs. One is also looking at crops that generate cash for the smallholder, as opposed to subsistence farming where the peasant consumes nearly all that he produces and never breaks out of the poverty cycle.

There is also one marvellous initiative called "Peace Gardens" which encourages the establishment of small vegetable plots in existing rural and urban communities. Again the market is close at hand. Moreover, it is extraordinary how small a viable plot can be with the right seeds and methods of cultivation. It's the size of a front door!

Men are smarter than women

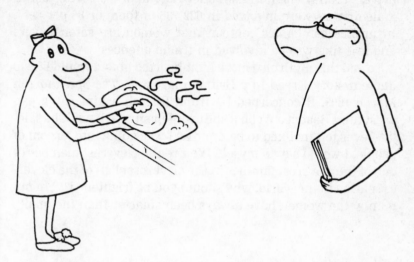

Physically stronger, maybe, but smarter – that's a hoary chestnut of a myth in South Africa. It's quite extraordinary how at any dinner party one goes to, the men huddle in conversation in one clump before the meal and the women in another. Perhaps it's not a symbol of male chauvinism (just common interests) but a telling sign is that there are fewer women proportionately in frontline positions in politics and business here than in Western societies.

Once South Africa has made the transition to a more normal, nonracial condition, gender discrimination – which has forever been overshadowed by colour discrimination – will become a much hotter issue. One hopes that we don't emulate the other traditionally male stronghold of Australia in spawning an aggressive feminist movement to counteract the inequalities. It would be better to see women take their rightful place in society through individual advancement on merit rather than by heavy-handed lobbying. Given the overriding problem of violence in this country, women can be a far more effective force for peace than men because of their greater concern for creating a society in which their children are not at peril.

A subsidiary myth in South Africa is that men are better drivers than women. In 1991, out of a total of 749 224 accidents, male drivers were involved in 622 736 of them or 83 per cent. Insurance companies confirm that women are safer drivers and less likely to be involved in traffic offences.

To end this myth on a more light-hearted note, I would like to quote a story I read in a British magazine, *The Spectator*, in March 1993. It concerned Bertrand Russell asking my great-great-aunt Beatrice Webb if she ever felt shy. "Oh no," she said. "If I ever felt inclined to be timid as I was going into a room of people, I would say to myself, 'You're the cleverest member of one of the cleverest families in the cleverest class of the cleverest nation in the world, why should you be frightened?'" In my family, the women have always been smarter than the men!

Money grows on trees

This myth is strong among the nonbusiness segment of the South African population. Business is seen as a large mango tree. Give it a shake and ripe mangoes will rain down. Extra tax needed for government to spend on social programmes – shake the tree. Soft loans required for community housing – do the same. Additional levies wanted to fund a new government department – no problem. More money to cover stiffer environmental regulations – shake the tree a little harder. Universities, charities, community-action groups desperate for cash – how can they go away empty-handed? The list goes on and it's endless. Not that many of these requests in themselves are not eminently reasonable. They are. What gives business the feeling of being overwhelmed is the totality of demands – more and more outgoings on an industrial and commercial base that has been shrunk by the recession.

The other side of this myth is the belief amongst the clever people who make up the think-tanks for formulating future national economic strategies that the tree is easy to plant in the first place – and it can be made to bear fruit fast. The kind of "blah" that one hears so often is that this country must not go the low-wage, low-technology path of some Asian tigers. We must choose the high-wage, capital-intensive route of advanced European nations (and miraculously achieve full employment at the same time). As though the market is waiting with bated breath for high value-added products from the New South Africa, businessmen here are too flat-footed to see these glaring opportunities, and it merely needs a select group of highly intelligent economic experts to orchestrate these dumb businessmen to see the light! The "Let there be a new industry and it will create a million jobs" lobby is very strong among people who have never been entrepreneurs themselves.

The reality is that money is very hard to make these days in a world where a constant surplus of consumer goods has been created by the latest strides in technology. The books that offer 'x' easy ways to get rich conveniently forget that to obtain the reward, money has to be wagered and a firm judgement made of the probabilities of success or failure. Indeed the whole subject of calculating the risks and rewards of doing business is foreign to many of the so-called national strategists.

The best you can do as a government is to provide an environment that is truly favourable for entrepreneurs to grow and flourish. Then you let the people with the "nose" for business get on with it.

The strategists will lose a lot of money if they enter the casino of business and try to gamble themselves.

Crime doesn't pay

For an industry that doesn't pay, crime attracts a lot of new recruits! Ask any taxi driver in New York, Sydney, Rio de Janeiro, London or Moscow, and in each city he will say crime is soaring. Shoplifting, housebreaking, robbery with violence, robbery with murder, carjacking, sophisticated white-collar fraud – you name the criminal activity and look at the line on the graph. It slopes forever upwards. Then there are the big-time activities like the narcotics trade. Turnover in narcotics ranks it with tourism, defence and oil. On a bottom-line basis it is probably the most profitable industry in the world today. Profit before tax is profit after tax.

While crime has always been with us, it's been kept under control because the risks have outweighed the rewards. But over the last 50 years it's switched the other way round and the floodgates have opened. The logic of a criminal nowadays, when he compares his lot with preceding generations, is probably as follows: If I commit a crime, there's less chance of detection because the police force is overstretched. If I am detected I'll probably escape because I'm better armed than the policemen sent to arrest me. If I'm arrested, there's a good chance I'll get off the rap because of a smart lawyer. If I do take the rap, I'll probably only get a light sentence which with good behaviour will be lighter still.

More liberal thinking towards crime in most Western societies has led to less barbaric punishment. But criminals are every bit as barbaric and are now better armed and better organised than ever. Italy appears to be the one country which has had the courage to draw the line and arrest the leaders of the Mafia as well as thousands of corrupt politicians, local officials and businessmen. "Operation Clean Hands", as it is called in Italy, has the full backing of the Italian population.

In South Africa every decent person is desperately concerned about the crime wave. The PWV complex is reputed to have one of the highest murder rates in the world. Violence is keeping the tourists and potential investors away in droves. As well as the factors mentioned above, we have had the added dimension of politics making the role of the policeman as the public-spirited upholder of law and order virtually impossible. We have had the ambiguity in distinguishing political and criminal offenders which undermines the judicial system. The sooner we have a new government in place under which the South African Police receives wholehearted community support and no excuses can be made at all for criminal activity the better. The "all cops are bad" myth must be firmly dispelled. Ultimately, though, the strongest crime prevention measures are the resurrection of family values and the creation of jobs. As one American priest put it: "Nothing stops bullets like jobs." Until we're well on the way towards achieving the goal of millions of new jobs in the small business and informal sector, the rewards of crime will unfortunately continue to outweigh the risks for those with nothing to lose.

A good education guarantees you a job

Let's begin with a couple of examples to illustrate how fundamentally the job market has altered to cause this to be a myth.

A graduate with a degree with distinction in Engineering from Wits only obtained a job in Johannesburg recently when he dropped this fact from his curriculum vitae. He was then immediately hired as a draughtsman, and he intends telling his employer in a year's time that he actually has a degree and if there is any chance of promotion, perhaps they'll consider him. Times have changed. In the old days, people "embroidered" their CV to get a job interview. Now to get a foot in the door, they downgrade it so that they're not overqualified.

The second example comes from a visit I made to Australia early in 1993, during which I made a few scenario presentations in major cities concerning Australia's future (interesting, and there's a myth about the place elsewhere in the book). What I couldn't get over was the number of well-qualified graduates who were shattered by the realisation that the school certificates and university degrees that they had worked so hard for had no value in the marketplace. As children, they had misguidedly put their faith in the system created by the adults around them – their parents, their teachers, their university professors. They thought they were working for some meaningful goal; it proved an illusion.

We have a situation now where the world of education and the world of business are totally out of "sync" with one another. There's no awareness in the teaching and educational fraternity of the revolution in the structure of the labour market. Part of this is due to the fact that many influential educationists have a natural antipathy towards capitalism and the profit motive, which is why they joined their profession in the first place. They're shaping the educational system according to their image of the world as it ought to be – not as it is. The system then churns out unemployable students with zero prospects in the real world.

One thing is for sure. The market is not going to change to accommodate the educational system. It is going to have to be the other way around. So what has happened to the labour market? The answer lies in one statistic: 95 per cent of the jobs being created worldwide are in the small business and informal sector. Go to America or Britain. The fastest growing sector of employment in both these countries is self-employment and temporary or part-time work (I categorise the last two as "informal" because the people concerned do not normally quai for the benefits offered in the formal sector). The number ot permanent employees in big business is shrinking everywhere, partially due to automation (machine tools, robots, personal computers, etc.) and partially due to outsourcing (more and more activities done in-house are being subcontracted to small independent companies). Governments worldwide are feeling the pinch and have either frozen their civil services or are cutting them down. The days are gone when one could simply get a good degree from university and glide effortlessly into the public service or a management traineeship in the private sector. Thirty years ago I did Latin and Greek at school and medieval philosophy at university and knew I was going to get a job. I wonder what I would do now?

The world of education and the world of business will have to move a lot closer in order to overcome the incredible mismatch that lies between them at the moment. For starters, schools will need to stop educating children to be employees, and instead encourage them to be employers (of themselves and if successful of others too). The current system of assembling children in a classroom to listen to an adult for forty-five minutes and then sending them to another classroom for another collective but passive experience hardly qualifies them for the proactive role they need to play in marketing themselves in the commercial world afterwards. Is there one South African school that is running classes in how to be an entrepreneur and open up your own business as part of its core curriculum?

Unemployment is cyclical

Many people think of unemployment as a cyclical phenomenon purely related to business activity. According to this myth, most of the 35 million or so currently unemployed in the rich nations, and the hundreds of millions unemployed elsewhere, will automatically find jobs as soon as the global economy starts to expand again. However, just like the out-of-touch educationists, the economic commentators who make this kind of projection have entirely misread the fundamental restructuring of the labour market. Unless attitudes to work change in a far-reaching way, many of the casualties of the recent recession will be permanently without a job.

We have been through two hundred years of concentrating workers into ever-larger units of production through the process of industrialisation. Economies of scale have made it relatively easy to pack hundreds of thousands of unskilled people on mass-production lines doing simple repetitive manual tasks. But, with the bargaining power of unions pushing up the cost of this labour, large companies have been motivated for a long time to substitute machines for people. The alternative has been to locate labour-intensive plants in countries where the wages are still low compared to the world average. This trend is called the "hollowing-out of industry" in Western countries. Hence, in the last twenty years, the enormous strides in manufacturing productivity and spreading of manufacturing networks of large companies throughout the world have made the concept of mass employment obsolete in the rich countries. Gone are the days when youthful but unqualified job seekers could, with comparative ease, pick up a humble post on an assembly line.

Any new project these days – a new steel mill, a new colliery, a new car plant – hires only a tiny fraction of the people they used to hire, and the successful applicants have to be much better qualified than they used to be. Moreover, the wonders of new technology have made it possible to circumvent the principle of economies of scale and produce goods cheaply in small batches. In broad macro terms, therefore, we are moving from a society where masses of people were employed in huge workforces under single factory roofs to one where small units of highly knowledgeable employees are supervising, monitoring and maintaining sophisticated machines.

So where will the rest go? The answer is that, for the majority of any country's population in future, we will have to return to the highly dispersed pattern of employment that existed prior to the industrial revolution. Cottage industries – simple low-technology ones and sophisticated high-technology ones – will become the order of the day. At least the latest advances in tele-communication which allow business to be done from the home (telecommuting) will facilitate this evolution in work patterns. One of the reasons why countries like Malaysia and Indonesia are doing so well now is that their fabric of villages was never destroyed by industrialisation or urbanisation. The self-sufficient village with self-motivated villagers (not beholden to the state) endures. Community work ethic is high. When this is combined with appropriate modern technology in agriculture and small home industries, the results are very effective.

An example I'm more familiar with is my mother's village, a place called Midhurst in West Sussex, England. (Incidentally, some of the villagers have never been to London which is only 75 miles away!) Despite the recession in the UK as a whole, the village has remained relatively unscathed. Each villager has a role to play, and many of the roles have been handed down from father to son – teacher, doctor, lawyer, fishmonger, grocer, fur-niture maker, woodsman, farmer and inn-keeper. Additional roles have been added over time, like dry-cleaner, television repairer, car mechanic and video hirer. One old fellow carries around a couple of canisters on his back containing liquid ferti-lizer plus a very tall nozzle emanating vertically from the canis-ters to a height several times his own. He is the official waterer of the flower boxes of the village's cottages and shops!

Recently, a supermarket chain wanted to establish a large store on the outskirts of the village about which there were very mixed feelings from the villagers themselves. Everybody knew that a development of this nature would lead to closure of the smaller village shops. This in turn would disrupt communal life by eliminating some long-standing occupations (possibly in ex-change for low-ranking posts in the supermarket chain) and by making shopping more inconvenient and less friendly, particu-larly for the infirm and elderly (the village store being the gos-sip centre). Anyway, the project never went ahead, but it repre-sents an interesting dilemma which will be repeated time and time again. Should one be guided by economic rationality and in this case accept a project which will definitely lead to lower prices on the shelves for consumers, or does one take into account the social costs of disruption which would make the decision go the other way? This is exactly what, on a much broader scale, Europe is debating as it faces the highest unemployment levels in its history with little prospect of new job creation in the near future. On the one hand, most economists argue (quite rightly) in favour of free trade, but on the other hand massive social unrest as a result of unemployment could bring whole societies down.

Not far away from Midhurst across the Surrey border is the town of Haslemere which is located on the main railway line from Portsmouth to London. Many of its inhabitants commute to London daily – or did until the recession took away their jobs. It is doubtful whether many of those made redundant will find jobs again in London, and so they're having to fend for themselves by attempting to open up small businesses or become business consultants locally. Unfortunately, some have no option but to live off their private means whilst telling their friends they are merely between jobs. The contrast between the economies of Midhurst and Haslemere – one reasonably in shape and the other suffering under the recession – demonstrates how vulnerable communities become when they are too dependent on forces outside their control (in Haslemere's case the London economy which in turn reflects the state of the world economy).

We are moving into a two-speed world. On the one hand products like television sets, video cassette recorders and cars will be produced by world-class companies with global manufacturing facilities. Villages are not going to compete with big business in these categories. On the other hand, millions of niche markets in home industries are going to be exploited by a new class of village entrepreneurs. The majority of the world's population will be employed in the second category, and those countries which identify and encourage these new trends in employment will be the ones with the lowest unemployment rates. For example, if a government is intending to pursue a job-creation programme, it will be more successful in accomplishing its aims if it provides financial assistance to communities to establish their own mini-enterprise networks as opposed to undertaking national public works programmes.

There is also an important philosophical implication to the changes described above. We are not going to be as rich as we were before. If the old material aspirations persist, we shall have many dissatisfied children who see that they are worse off than their parents. Society is going to have to go through cold turkey where, for many, having a job is a means for survival – it is no longer a stairway to expensive luxuries and treats. There is no alternative!

There is an ideal democracy

No democracy is perfect. That's a myth. But a quotable quote is that democracy is the least worst system man has discovered to govern a nation. The reason for this is that absolute power corrupts absolutely, which is the tendency in dictatorships or authoritarian regimes. Democracy, while it never eliminates corruption completely, is a way of minimising it. Corrupt politicians – provided they're exposed by an independent press – can be booted out at the next election.

There are many working models of democracy, each with its strengths and weaknesses. It can be backed by a written constitution (America) or an unwritten tradition (Britain). Nevertheless, some common strands to good democracies are emerging. Firstly, multi-party democracies function better than one-party democracies (if there is such a thing!). Secondly, certain institutions are independent of government, such as the judiciary, the central bank and the press. Thirdly, the maximum term of an elected government lies between three and five years: less than that range, the government's thinking is too short-term because the next election is always around the corner; longer than that range, the government is being held accountable for its results too infrequently. Fourthly, parliament consists of two houses. The lower house tends to be the "democratic" one which most reflects the voting patterns of the people, while the upper one is elected or chosen on the basis that it should act as a check on the lower house by delaying, moderating or even vetoing its decisions.

The differences between democracies are equally important. Does one have a ceremonial head of state (the monarch in Britain, president in Germany) or an executive head of state sharing power with the legislature (America) or "cohabiting" with a prime minister (France)? Where the position of head of state is ceremonial, the chief executive (prime minister in Britain, chancellor in Germany) has a great deal of personal power to get things done. Where there is power sharing, checks and balances ensure that executive authority is not abused. Does one elect a party to govern using the first-past-the-post, Westminster method, or proportional representation, or something in between? First-past-the-post has the advantage of a bad government being totally replaced at the next election, but the disadvantage of majority rule to the exclusion of minorities. Proportional representation has the advantage of more representative government (coalitions are the norm), but the disadvantages of little change at each election and fringe parties playing too decisive a role by threatening to walk out of coalitions. The last two points are the reason why the Italians have voted to switch to a system principally featuring first-past-the-post.

The final difference in democracies concerns the relationship which the regions that make up a nation bear to the central government, ranging from the loosest form (a confederation in Switzerland) through a looser form (a federation in America, Canada, Australia) to the tightest form (a unitary state in Britain and France). On the one hand, having regional governments allows a greater degree of latitude for local people to decide their own lives, but on the other hand every additional layer of government means more bureaucrats, which means more taxes.

Democracy is therefore like a suit. It has to be tailored to fit the unusual characteristics and preferences of each nation. Formulators of a new constitution for South Africa – take note. Don't search endlessly for the ideal democracy. Be practical.

Class is disappearing

Bunkum! George Orwell made the most famous comment about class when he said: "All animals are equal but some animals are more equal than others." Mankind (and this even includes socialists) has a natural predisposition for hierarchies. So, whatever country you travel to, you will find some form of class system. In Britain, class is principally determined by birth, in America by money and birth (if you are born a Kennedy you have a major head start!), in France by intellect, in India by caste.

A class system is no bad thing for a country provided it is not taken so far that it becomes divisive. For example, in Britain the "we-they" attitude that exists between management and workers has bedevilled industrial relations and has therefore impaired the performance of British industry. It is no coincidence that some of the best-run companies achieving the best results in Britain today are owned and managed by the Japanese. Indeed, following their economic success of the last 20 years, the latter probably come closest to being a one-class nation – middle class.

In South Africa, we have several kinds of class system. In Johannesburg money is what counts whether it is new or old, but in Cape Town it can only be old money! One can say with absolute certainty that these class divisions will remain, the only difference being that each class will become increasingly nonracial. For that reason, the continuation of class could have some benefits in that it horizontally cuts across the deep vertical divides of language and race. But a cautionary word is in order. The borders between the classes must never become barriers to advancement. The great charm of the American system is that the most humbly born person can aspire to be a billionaire or the president.

If I don't go to university
I must be a failure

South Africa has inherited this terrible myth from Britain. One of the great tragedies of British society is how British intellectual snobbery has over the past 150 years downgraded the value of manual skills. In the late 18th and early 19th centuries, when Britain was riding the crest of the industrial wave, being a craftsman and belonging to a guild were attributes that were highly respected. Manufacturing thrived because it attracted some of the brightest and the best on account of its exciting pioneering image. Interestingly, few of the inventors who contributed so much to the Industrial Revolution by creating marvellous machines like the flying shuttle, the power loom, the steam engine and the steam locomotive went to Oxford or Cambridge, and most of them were Scots. One can therefore say with a fair degree of confidence that Britain's greatness was due to a clever bunch of nongraduates!

Various trends conspired to cause manufacturing in Britain to be viewed in a more negative light. The children of the original mill owners had a more genteel education than their parents and were less inclined to get their hands dirty. Influential societies, such as the Fabian Society and later the Bloomsbury Group, put a premium on intellect over craftmanship (ironic since many of those intellectuals claimed to be supporters of the working class). Schools and universities allocated an increasing proportion of their curricula to the arts and humanities instead of science and mathematics. Finally, the new-found prosperity boosted the status of occupations such as law and finance so that the best and the brightest flocked into them rather than manufacturing.

The consequences of this denigration of "using one's hands" and "producing goods" have been disastrous for Britain: chronic unemployment, loss of competitiveness and a depreciating currency. No Chancellor of the Exchequer, however brilliant, could have kept the pound in a narrow band with the other Common Market currencies – it is stupid to heap all the blame on him. Japan and Germany followed precisely the opposite route after the Second World War, laying great emphasis on manufacturing. Germany in particular focused on practical-skills training and apprenticeship schemes in order to attain the highest level of engineering standards in the world.

In South Africa, the value of technikons and technical colleges has been totally underrated. We have more graduates than diplomates in science, which is crazy when one considers that the Asian tigers have exactly the opposite. Politicians in the past even implied that because practical-skills training was inferior, the vast bulk of the population should be consigned to it (the ultimate snobbism!). This means that virtually every child, black and white, in South Africa wants a university education. Not only is this impossible, it is unwise. As explained under the myth "Unemployment is cyclical", the jobs are simply not available.

But to go to the heart of the myth, the idea that only graduates are successes later in life is arrant nonsense. Plenty of people who never saw the inside of a university have made major contributions to society here. Moreover, a powerful subsidiary

myth for many South African youngsters is that to get anywhere you need to go into politics, the civil service, law or some
other profession. This attitude could turn into a huge millstone
around the country's neck.

To lay this myth to rest, let me tell a story about a most enter-
prising coloured lady living near Cape Town, who started her
own business in the rag trade. She purchased for a total of
R5 000 a second-hand cloth-cutting table, a cutting knife, three
irons and a machine to sew on buttons. She then went to about
150 seamstresses who have their own sewing machines and entered into contracts with each of them whereby she supplies the
cut material and they sew each dress together for between R6,50
and R8,50 per dress. She collects the dresses, sews on the buttons, presses them and checks them for quality defects. Finally,
in her bedroom, which she has converted into a showroom, she
markets these dresses to agents and hawkers who buy in lots of
10 to 20 dresses. The upshot of this arrangement is that the
seamstresses earn between R250 and R500 a week, with some of
them occasionally hitting a peak of R750, compared with an industry minimum of R212 a week. They save money on transport
because they work at home, and their productivity has risen
because they decide on their own working hours (some work at
night). The customers are more than satisfied with the arrangement because the prices of her dresses are very competitive.
But the real kicker is that the profit of her business varies between R35 000 and R50 000 per month. That's quite a return on a
capital employed of R5 000! The reason that she has turned a
marginal activity in the formal sector into a highly profitable
business in the informal sector is the shedding of overheads
and the spreading of capital investment into many hands. The
point of this example is that the lady in question never got beyond Standard 8, and yet she has achieved what thousands of
graduates only dream of.

Art should be PC – politically correct

Homer, Elvis Presley, William Shakespeare, Louis Armstrong, Michelangelo, Marlon Brando, Wolfgang Amadeus Mozart, Emily Brontë, Bob Marley, John Lennon, Charles Dickens and Ella Fitzgerald – I selected these names at random from all fields of art.

What do they have in common? They were all great entertainers. People read their poems and stories, listen to their voices and music, look at their paintings, sculptures, movies and plays to be transported out of themselves. The Greek word "catharsis" – a cleansing of the soul – comes closest to the main objective of any art form. But the senses have to be stimulated in order for the soul to be cleansed. If there was a political message in the works of any of these great artists, it was subtly disguised, it was put across in an oblique manner.

Too much of today's art pursues the myth of trying to be PC first and entertaining second. The more clumsy the protest the less captivating the content. If it's too PC, people automatically smell a rat. They won't buy the book or go to see the play. If it's put on television, they'll tune to another channel – particularly in a few years' time when cheap satellite dishes will make it possible to receive any number of international stations in any country. There's always the video shop as well.

Another PC myth, prevalent in America and South Africa, is to divide art into Eurocentric and Afrocentric categories. In 1988 Nick Green and Reg Lascaris wrote a ground-breaking book called *Third World Destiny*, in which they exposed the myth of dividing up the market into racial categories for advertising purposes. The authors convincingly demonstrated that the market is free of racial bias and should therefore be analysed into bands based on educational and income levels alone. In a broader way, they showed that a crossover culture is developing in South African society and the pigeonholing of con-

sumer goods, newspapers, radio stations and television channels into those favoured by whites and those favoured by blacks
is generally an archaic notion. This applies to art too – PC is
definitely BC!

If I win you lose

Most children are brought up to accept this myth as a major principle of life. School cricket, rugby and football matches testify to this logic (unless there is a draw!). When the prefects are chosen, you may be in but your friend is out. At school prizegiving, if your rival is a prizewinner you may be part of the rest who are not. When you are a little older, you win the girl you love or you lose her to someone else. In business, if you're gaining market share another company must be losing its. If you get promoted your office colleague may be left behind. At bridge, poker or monopoly, if I win you lose. They're zero-sum games, i.e. if I am plus one rand, you must be minus one rand, and the net result is zero.

In order to show that there are exceptions to this principle, let's flash back to the Olympic Games at Barcelona when Elana

Meyer came second in the final of her race. She accepted her loss so graciously by embracing the Ethiopian winner that she'll be remembered more for that than if she had won the race. At home, I recently watched a first-team rugby match between St John's and St Stithian's which St Stithian's won 13-10. It was thrilling to watch because both teams gave of their best but displayed excellent decorum. For many of the crowd there were no losers, just 30 marvellous young players in a roller coaster of a spectacle. However, I also know that, given the strength of the myth, the preceding comments are small consolation to the St John's boys.

Had you been lucky enough to have gone to one of the better preprimary schools, you would have been introduced to the concepts of teamwork and win-win at a very early age. By performing tasks together, the children soon learn that they can accomplish more than they can by selfishly working for themselves (prima donnas take note!).

The same philosophy drives any sound negotiation process. The parties deal with the issues in a joint problem-solving manner rather than with the attitude of "I'll give as little as possible and take as much as I can". Anyway, negotiators who try to grab everything often leave the table with nothing.

In the game of life, in contrast to poker, in order to win one must turn others into winners too. I remember seeing a sign on a manager's desk which plaintively asked: "How can I soar like an eagle when I am surrounded by turkeys?" The correct reply is: "By turning those turkeys into eagles too."

Education is for six- to twenty-two-year-olds

Conferences on the future of education examine primary, secondary and university education to the nth degree. The state and various charities direct most of their money to educational institutions at these three levels. By comparison, you seldom come across a serious gathering on the topic of education on either side – nursery schools and kindergartens on the one hand and adult education on the other. Hardly ever are serious fund-raising drives mounted for these two almost forgotten phases of education, and the state provides little finance for them.

Let's start at the very beginning. In France, a comprehensive study recently showed that children who start schooling as young as two and a half years old perform better in examinations in later years than children who begin the learning process at primary school. Similar conclusions have been arrived at in Britain and the US. In other words, preprimary schooling can give a child a critical head start in language skills, learning about numbers and getting along with other children. Such schooling should not be regarded merely as a crèche where mothers can leave their children during the day while they work. It is much more than that, particularly as the pressures of modern life have diminished the opportunities for children to socialise within the family group.

At the other end of the scale a nation's education system should have the flexibility to cater for mature students – from those who want to learn basic literacy to those who need to acquire new job skills if they've been made redundant to others who simply want to improve their knowledge by taking further degrees. In this ever-changing world, adults ought to have the opportunity of going back to school.

It is wrong to place less emphasis on the education of under 6-year-olds and over 22-year-olds than on the education of those in between. Although South Africa currently possesses many brilliant organisations which are plugging the gaps, the subjects of infant and adult education should be seen as coequals to normal schooling. As I said in my original "High Road" presentation in 1986, the three most important conditions of a winning nation are education, education and education (provided it is relevant). That means education for life.

Words are read

Billions of words are being written each day in newspapers, magazines, books, letters, telexes, facsimiles, office internal memoranda and now electronic mail. The world is awash with words. Concurrently, other ways of obtaining information and of being entertained are becoming increasingly available to consumers. Radio (more stations), television (more channels) and video are just three ways of diverting the market away from the written word. Consequently, more manuscripts, articles and memoranda are skimmed through instead of read than ever before. For the writer, this places an even higher premium on brevity and relevance than heretofore. Nowadays the title and the first paragraph really count!

Another myth revolves around the number of people who can read and do read. In America and Britain, because of declining educational standards, a growing number of school-leavers (and, amazingly, university graduates) cannot grasp the theme of even the most straightforward article. Only one half of the adult US population purchase a daily newspaper. This means that the chattering classes – the people who do read the newspapers and chatter to one another over the dinner table about what they've read – seriously overestimate the size of the constituency that shares their ideas and opinions about the issues of the day. In parallel, the print media itself commits the same mistake. So when the population at large diverges in its behaviour from the predictions of the chattering classes, the informed observers write with shock and dismay about how current events have gone completely against the trend.

In South Africa, one needs only to listen to talk shows on the radio and read the letter columns of newspapers to realise how wide the gap sometimes is between the views of the man in the street and those of the chattering classes. The results of the first truly democratic election may well confound the seasoned political experts, just as the results of the last referendum on continuing negotiations did, when the fears of the chattering classes about a swing to the right proved unfounded. For the time being, the best form of mass communication in South Africa will remain the radio.

Booze buys manhood

In addressing this myth I am not about to preach that South Africa should become a dry society. This myth is about the abuse, not the use, of alcohol. It is considered "macho" by a section of the young population in this country to get absolutely smashed (or "axed" in current parlance) on a regular basis. Overseas, such young people are called "lager louts". Not only does overdrinking lead to totally unacceptable behaviour, it causes many road accidents involving the deaths of innocent people.

It is extraordinary how far South Africa lags behind Australia, Britain and other countries in applying really strict measures against drunken driving. Overseas, random stopping of drivers for breathalyser tests, withdrawal of licences for extended periods and jail sentences are the order of the day – they've been very effective in cutting down the number of accidents and road deaths. In some states in America, legal action can even be taken against bartenders and hosts if they allow someone to drive home who they know is over the limit. Here, ludicrously low fines have in the past been levied on the guilty. In one newspaper, not so long ago, the sentence imposed on a drunken driver who killed a pedestrian was milder than that imposed on a thief who had stolen bread from a café. The carnage goes on.

Moreover, virtually nothing is done in South Africa to stop underage drinking in public places. Very few bars and clubs ask young people to show identification to prove their age.

The real problem of binge-drinking youngsters is that they become hard-drinking adults. They lose their jobs, they mess up their marriages and the lives of their children. They become a liability to society and cause untold unhappiness to themselves. Some may be lucky enough to be helped back to a normal life by one of the splendid groups involved in the rehabilitation of alcoholics. But it is a long, hard road that the young do not appreciate.

Some drugs aren't dangerous

It is a myth to draw a distinction between softer drugs like marijuana and harder drugs like heroin and call for the legalisation of the softer ones. Bearing in mind the current consumption of alcohol and cigarettes among teenagers, experts estimate that if softer drugs were legalised their use would at least triple overnight. The argument that kids are at present more attracted to drugs because they are prohibited just does not hold water. There is a huge pool of law-abiding people out there who might be tempted to experiment with certain drugs but don't because they are illegal.

Moreover, a drug like marijuana is called a "gateway drug". As a user becomes addicted to its hallucinogenic properties, he is remorselessly drawn on from its occasional use to obtain pleasurable experiences to having to take the drug to satisfy a psychological dependency. His tolerance to the drug rises and he seeks a greater variety of experience from harder drugs. Eventually, the mind or the body snaps and the options become rehabilitation, lingering on in a no-man's land or death. Alcoholism follows a similar deadly course – hence the term "substance abuse" to cover both drugs and alcohol.

So why not, as those who seek to overturn the prohibition of drug usage contend, treat drugs in the same way as alcohol and use social pressures to restrain people from substance abuse? Then we could get the criminals who tempt people to switch to harder, more profitable drugs out of the distribution system. The answer is that drugs, unlike alcohol, still have a huge number of potential consumers waiting in the wings. If drugs are unbanned they can never be banned again if it proves to be a mistake. Prohibition of alcohol in America demonstrated the futility of trying to reverse something that the public has come to consider socially acceptable.

There is no work ethic in South Africa

A story which has been around for years is of a company chairman taking a visitor around his head office. On being asked by his guest how many people worked there, he responded: "About 50 per cent!" The other favourite is of a conversation between the chief of South African Railways and the head of a large company in which they were comparing relative size. They went through assets, profits, labour force and other yardsticks and every time SAR came out on top. But finally the company head wryly said: "There's one category where we are ahead of you. We carry more passengers!"

Despite these stories and the generally held belief that South Africa does not possess a work ethic, the truth is that large segments of the population work extremely hard. This is particularly apparent among the entrepreneurs in the townships who have no welfare system to fall back on and no "the world owes me a living" type of attitude. In my case I think of the hundreds of thousands of miners who go underground every day and work under the most arduous conditions. I wouldn't exchange them for any other mining workforce anywhere in the world. I am sure that many other chief executives would say the same about their employees. The shakedown of industry due to the recent recession has improved productivity immeasurably. South Africa is beginning to hold its head high again in many export fields. Free lunches are a rarity these days and those absolutely essential overseas trips have vanished!

However, one cloud looms ominously on the horizon – affirmative action of the wrong kind where it just turns into a parasitical jobs-for-pals programme. Head offices will swell, the civil service will triple and government expenditure will zoom to 60 per cent of GDP, if not higher. The beneficiaries are paid for putting their feet on the desk and looking out of the window. I was so glad to be rid of this gravy-train mentality when I left England. There it is called the "old boy network", which is in reality a clubby affirmative-action programme for those of the upper classes who can't get jobs in the open market. Heaven preserve us from a similar fate in South Africa!

The informal sector is peripheral

In the past, the informal sector has been described as a refugee camp from the formal sector. It is only the discards from the latter that go into the former, and in an ideal world everyone would work in the formal sector. In disposing of the myth "Unemployment is cyclical", I made it plain that this dream is unattainable.

However, to demonstrate that the development of microbusiness is central, and not peripheral, to a positive future for South Africa, I would like to recount a story about a Durban man involved in the import-export business who went out on a worldwide tender for new steak knives. He settled on a Japanese company which, besides satisfying the Japanese domestic market, exported 32 million steak knives a year to the US. By any standards, this was a large company. Nevertheless, before signing the contract he decided to fly to Tokyo to meet the management personally and inspect the operation. He went to a nice head-office building in the central district and was impressed by the politeness and efficiency of the staff he met. Yet, whenever he asked to see the plant producing the knives, the management would immediately change the subject and suggest they accompany him to a geisha bar or a shrine. On the final day of his visit, he put his foot down and said he would not sign the contract until he saw the plant.

The managing director rather shamefacedly put him in his car and drove him to the outskirts of Tokyo where they stopped at an open lot with a small shack on it. The MD walked with his guest to the shack and opened the door. Inside was an old man with a 1950s machine in superb working order used to press out stainless steel blanks. Taken aback, the Durban man asked if that was all. No, was the response, this unit was repeated a thousand times around Tokyo – each pressing out steel blanks. The MD then went on to describe the rest of the production process. There was a similar number of units shaping the blanks into the form of a blade, another lot sharpening the blades, another lot making the copper pins to fasten the blades to the handle, another lot fashioning the handles and finally another lot assembling the knives. All of these operations were independent microbusinesses contracted to do highly specific tasks. The Durban man asked how the components were transported between units. The Japanese MD showed him a fleet of little motorbikes with boxes on the back. They were the link! The only operation that the company itself owned was a warehouse where the knives were packed in presentation boxes and loaded into shipping containers. Quality control was exercised at this stage.

The point of this story is that the Durban man's conception of a company producing this size of output was one that had a modern plant backed up by all kinds of departments providing ancillary services. Every stage of the process would be owned and controlled by the company. The Japanese MD, sensing the amazement of his client, said that the networking approach that he had seen was developed by Japan after the Second World War to break into the global market. Given that Japan at the time had not built up a reputation for quality, the only way it could gain market share was by undercutting the prices of competitors. This in turn meant ultra-specialisation at the microbusiness level with minimal overheads and with the ownership of capital assets diffused amongst many enterprises. The MD added that, despite the emergence of gigantic companies, the reality in Japan today was little different to the 1950s. Six out of seven Japanese work in small businesses, and large companies contract out a major part of their component manufacture to them. Because failure is not considered a bad thing in Japan, the country has the highest bankruptcy rate in the world as entrepreneurs try again and again to establish themselves in these networks.

The Durban man signed the contract. For South Africans in the formal sector, this story has a critical message: stop treating the informal sector as a fringe activity which should be handled as part of a social responsibility programme. Treat the forging of links between big and small business as a commercially serious venture which in the longer term may lead to greater efficiencies in your business. The spin-off will of course be extra jobs in the townships, directly through the placing of contracts and indirectly through the multiplier effect of greater disposable income circulating in the community.

Lastly, a myth prevalent in the central business district of the major South African cities is that hawkers hurt shops. Tension has therefore built up between the two. In fact, hawkers have a positive impact on retail activity because they represent a significant proportion of the turnover of shops that sell goods that can be hawked, i.e. the hawkers use the shops as wholesalers. More generally they attract potential customers to the CBDs, especially when they are gathered together in flea markets such as the one on Greenmarket Square in Cape Town.

Stay forever young

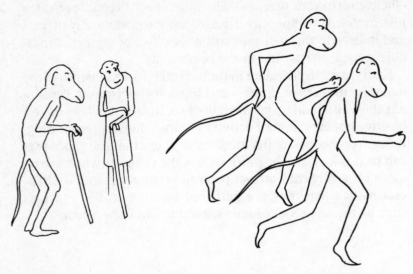

The cosmetics industry, plastic surgeons and aerobic instructors rely on this myth remaining strong. A socialite in the 1930s remarked: "A woman can never be too thin or too rich." But the march of age is relentless – from "wrinkly" to "trembly" to "crumbly" (terms used by the young to describe the phases of decline!).

If individuals wish to preserve the myth by any means at their disposal, that is their prerogative. However, the myth becomes dangerous when society as a whole views old age in a negative light, when ageing is seen as a reluctant surrender to the arrow of time instead of a road which opens up new opportunities, and when people grow old unwillingly and despondently instead of graciously and productively. Marketing deifies youth and the youth has lost respect for the wisdom and experience of older people. As a result, so much talent is going to waste in the community. For example, inexperienced entrepreneurs are crying out for mentors with knowledge of accounting, marketing and other functions of business. These mentorships could easily be undertaken by retired business people. If community projects multiply in future, they will need experienced, but inexpensive, managers. Again, the obvious source of such skills is the older generation.

The futile pursuit of retaining physical youth espoused so enthusiastically by articles and advertising in glossy magazines condemns many human beings to spend their middle age on a wretched treadmill. What use is a disappointed mind in a body which may fleetingly look like a thirtysomething?

Unity! Unity! Unity!

Whenever a politician calls for unity one has to treat it with the same suspicion as when he says, for instance, "Trust me", "Power to the people" or "You'll get the benefit but someone else will pay the tax". Unity on whose terms? His of course!

It's a myth to believe that a healthy society should display complete unity. In the real world, progress in any field is made through a permanent collision of opinions. Ideas are put up, debated, looked at from all sides and compared with other options. Slowly one wends one's way towards the truth. Sometimes, however, a government makes decisions that are plainly wrong and needs to be replaced. Hence, the presence of parties opposing the government is crucial for a properly functioning democracy. An opposition is not an enemy of the state, as some of those in power are prone to imply from time to time – it is just as loyal as those governing, but its views on good government differ.

I've always maintained that it's the second election that will count in the New South Africa, not the first election. The first one will be decided on emotion and history, but the second one will be decided on the effectiveness of the policies of the first government. A critical condition to ensure that the second election takes place is the formation of a nonpolitical army and police force, neither of which can be employed by a potential dictator to abolish the opposition and impose "unity" on his terms.

Incidentally, for small teams in business, sport and other activities, unity is a perfectly legitimate and feasible objective. It can even be applied to political parties, but not to the country as a whole.

Health at any cost

This myth is leading to a major smash in the health-delivery systems of most rich nations. Either health-care expenditure is soaring out of control where no ceilings exist (the US) or patient queues are remaining long where they do (the UK).

The causes are manifold: the ageing of the rich old millions which necessitates more intensive medical care for an increasing proportion of the population; the advancement in medical science involving new diagnostic techniques, new drugs, new methods of surgery, etc. which are often astronomically expensive; inefficiencies associated with the philosophy (of many governments) that if you throw money at the problem, you will solve it; rising insurance premiums paid by doctors to cover potential liabilities from errors of judgement; and a general escalation in the prices of outpatient and hospital care well ahead of the rate of inflation.

The net result is that governments everywhere are seeking to change the structure of the health industry to make delivery more economical. Medical aid societies are raising thresholds and lowering ceilings for financial assistance and qualifying their aid with more and more exclusions. Furthermore, companies are having to make enormous provisions for future medical liabilities of their present workforce and their dependants, together with pensioners and their wives.

In view of this crisis, which has been precipitated by the understandable belief of the medical profession that health care should be provided regardless of cost, preventive health care becomes an all-important method of keeping costs down. Primary health care should receive as much attention as keeping up with technological advances in hospitals. Above all, medical schools will need to include cost-benefit analysis as part of their curricula, since the balancing of optimal medical care against affordability is fast becoming the issue of the decade.

Warriors are the best role models

Kids these days are saturated with pictures of violence. Their heroes star in films like *Rambo*, *Die Hard*, *Lethal Weapon* and *Terminator*. They find martial art movies particularly riveting. When they come home from the cinema to watch television it is the same story – zap, pow, wham, boom and thud. As for a documentary on Mother Theresa – forget it! Now, on top of everything else, come computer games: the more graphic the method of ending the existence of the figures darting across the screen, the more popular the game. "Make my day", "Simple Simon Says" (SS being a Magnum pistol) – these are the phrases that resonate through their minds.

In real life, politicians whip up youthful audiences with militaristic metaphors about the struggle. Violence spills into the streets and schools. No wonder that kids believe that warriors are the best role models. No wonder that society is coming to resemble *Lord of the Flies*. If somebody crosses your path, obliterate him.

Thank goodness that kids also have sportsmen and women and pop stars as their role models, even though some of them are not exactly paragons of good manners. It is incumbent on the adult fraternity to address more seriously the challenge of providing alternative heroes and heroines for kids to emulate, and to show up violence for what it really is – sickening, gross and to be avoided at all costs.

Rights! Rights! Rights!

No. Obligations! Obligations! Obligations! The subject of human rights has so dominated the debate of what a decent society ought to be that the flip side – obligations – is never heard. Yet a recent sociological study of the most successful towns and villages in northern Italy (where "successful" was defined as having a high quality of life) revealed that it was not the richest centres that came out on top, but rather the ones which had the longest traditions of civic virtues. In other words, where townspeople or villagers felt a continuous sense of duty to help each other through hard times, the highest indices of communal happiness were recorded.

Rights are passive in that they stress what a person should receive and how he or she should be treated. Obligations are active in that they highlight what a person should do to qualify as an upright and honourable citizen. There is an old Eastern saying that if you want something really badly, it can only be achieved provided you have experienced the opposite state. To feel the pleasure of warmth, you have to come in from the cold. To be loved, you have to give love first. To enjoy comfort and ease, you must have worked hard to attain them. To appreciate wealth, you need to have known poverty. According to this logic, the conferment of rights on an individual can only occur once that individual has accepted his or her obligations to society. In short, rights and obligations are part of the same social contract.

A fine example of the "obligations" approach can be found in and around Stutterheim in the Eastern Cape. The local leaders from all communities – black, coloured and white – put their heads together to determine how they could overcome the ravages of the drought and the recession. They set up a range of joint forums covering areas like small-business development, agriculture, education and training. Action is now being taken in terms of the decisions made by the forums. Most importantly, jobs are being created. The antagonism and boycotts of the past have been replaced by an incredible spirit of "We're all in this together and we're obliged to help each other out". Brilliant! Stutterheim also demonstrates the power of assembling small teams and having tight feedback loops, e.g. raising money locally and spending it locally. There will always be much more transparency and accountability in communities which finance their own ventures, where everybody can keep an eye on each other, than in huge national initiatives administered by faceless bureaucrats.

In business the same principle of obligation applies. Management, employees and unions have all entered contracts with one another in which they're obliged to respect each other's interests and roles. Head office cannot rule by divine right, but neither can employees or unions unreasonably disrupt the business. The other day I was walking down a main haulage of one of the shafts of Freegold in the Orange Free State, Anglo's largest gold mine. Because of our policy of running each shaft as a business unit, the miners are very aware of the effect on profitability of variations in grade, changes in gold price and escalation of costs – in particular overhead costs. I was there-

119

fore not surprised when the mine overseer accompanying me casually remarked: "You know, meneer, down here we call you the Great Overhead!" In response, I mentioned a few examples where I felt Head Office (taking the "you" as collective!) had clearly added value to the operations at Freegold in the last year or so. Specifically I described the strategy devised at the centre to keep all of Freegold, including its marginal areas, running at full capacity. He seemed content with the answer, but what the incident showed is that just as he has an obligation to meet the tonnage called for underground from his section, we in Head Office have an obligation to provide an environment for him and his team which enables them to meet their targets. It's as simple as that!

Gold will bail us out again

Whenever there's an improvement in the gold price, it uplifts the spirit of most South Africans. Nothing wrong with that! One cannot deny that the gold mining industry has been the fly-wheel of the South African economy for a long time. Therefore any improvement in its prospects is bound to have widespread repercussions in a positive way for employment and economic activity.

The myth creeps in when politicians and businessmen treat the windfall of a higher gold price as the answer to all their prayers. Politicians meditate happily about the extra tax revenue which they will have to spend (or which will let them off the hook of a major budget deficit) while businessmen dream of the extra contracts that they will be awarded. Such fancies will merely lead to a re-run of the late 1970s and early 1980s in South Africa, when the boom in the gold market precipitated a waste-ful cycle of spending on projects which on anything approaching serious inspection would have been discarded as uneconomic.

Looking to the longer term, a nation's dependence on a single commodity can be a terrible handicap. Whether it's the Middle East with oil, Australia with wool and an array of other countries with tea, coffee, sugar, copper, etc., the story is similar in each of them: an economic boom when the price of the commodity is high and an economic bust when it isn't. The vulnerability and volatility of commodity-driven economies are not a solid base on which to build a prosperous and stable society.

It is no coincidence that the winning nations of this world are often those which have nothing but their wits to live on (hence the primacy of education). They buy the raw materials of other countries and add value to them. That added value tends to be more resilient to the ups and downs of the global economy than the profit margin on commodities.

The Japanese understood this reasoning a long time ago and therefore set themselves a target of manufacturing excellence which would propel them to the top of the league. Their gigantic trade surplus testifies to the success of this strategy. Yet, given the speed with which high technology is transferred between nations these days, more and more goods are being reclassified as commodities because of their universality – TV sets, cars, memory chips, etc. It becomes harder to find the niches where real value can be added as a result of the uniqueness of a product or service.

That is the challenge to South Africa's entrepreneurs: to find those profitable downstream niches. Nevertheless, the gold mining industry here still has plenty of life in it. With the strengthening of the jewellery market, particularly in the Far East, gold will continue to shine. All I say is: "Let a million other lights shine too!"

Customers are a nuisance

A quaint South African myth! Often when you walk into a shop, it's as though you as the customer are disturbing the peace and serenity of the assistants behind the counter. What right have you to be served! Government departments tend to become unhelpful when the lunch break is close at hand and telephone switchboards can leave you dangling on the end of the line if they're not putting you through to the wrong extension (whereafter you feel like a rugby ball as you are passed from one extension to another). Restaurants and hotels regard it as a favour to satisfy a customer's order. In plain English, South African society has a long way to go to become service-oriented. Ask any tourist.

It's always interested me that in the Marxist lexicon the word "customer" does not appear. This is because central planners presume that everything that is produced is automatically sold – you don't have to persuade people to buy things!

In Japan the customer is the centre of the universe – period.

South Africa is second-rate

The final myth is one that could psyche this country out of taking the "High Road" – the feeling that, no matter what this country does, the place is second-rate compared to other nations starring in the world today. All the negative propaganda over the years about South Africa from local as well as foreign sources appears to have made South Africans stop believing in themselves. What a tragedy it would be if just as we re-enter the world arena, the brightest and the best decide to follow their colleagues who have already left and relocate themselves and their families to other lands.

This country has the potential to astonish the world. There are so many initiatives going on at the moment at community level which in an unpublicised way are breaking all stereotypes. Whenever I get that feeling of glumness about the future because of something I've read in the press or experienced in real life, I focus on all the incredible individuals – friends, colleagues, acquaintances – that I have come across in these critical years. I say to myself, what a privilege to be in the same boat and to share the same hopes and fears.

Probably the most significant pointer that we are going to make it into the top league of nations on earth is the fact that tragedy in this country serves to bind people together rather than drive them apart – whether it's the assassination of Chris Hani, the murder of innocent members of the congregation of St James Church in Kenilworth or all the other appalling day-to-day happenings. Perhaps it's divine justice but to reach the goal of happiness, one has to experience misery and wretchedness first.

One last story to drive the clouds of anxiety away and bring a smile to the lips. On one particular course for budding entre-preneurs held in the townships, the students are told to turn up at 8 am sharp on the final day to collect their certificates. At 8 am the door is firmly closed and those who have not arrived by then are not allowed in. These latter unfortunates then divide themselves into two categories – those who shrug their shoulders and walk away, and those who bang on the doors and windows to be let in. If the banging goes on for 20 minutes, they are indeed allowed in on the grounds that they have an essen-tial quality to become an entrepreneur: perseverance!

That applies to everybody in this marvellous land. We are all pilgrims setting sail to an unknown destination. But with per-severance and courage, we shall all arrive safely and savour the thought that we destroyed the myth that South Africa is not the best place in the world to be.

Set in 10 on 13 pt Monotype Nimrod
Printed and bound by National Book Printers,
Goodwood, Cape, South Africa